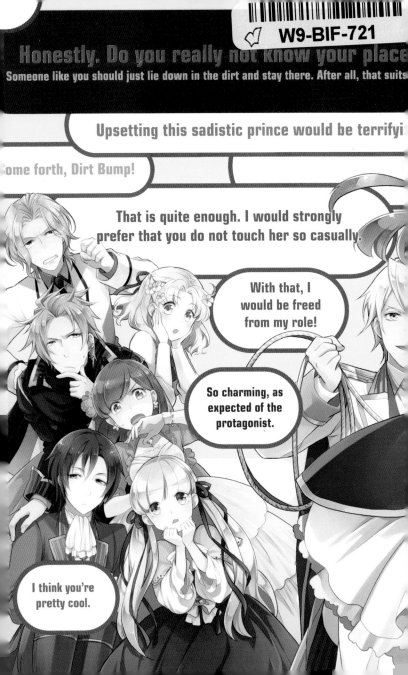

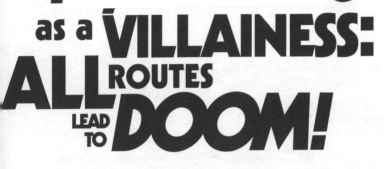

as a VILLAINESS: ALL ROUTES LEAD TO DOOM!

VOLUME 3

SATORU YAMAGUCHI
ILLUSTRATIONS BY NAMI HIDAKA

My Next Life as a Villainess: All Routes Lead to Doom! Volume 3
by Satoru Yamaguchi

Translated by Shirley Yeung
Edited by Aimee Zink
Manga Lettering by Kimberly Pham

Copyright © 2016 Satoru Yamaguchi
Illustrations by Nami Hidaka

First published in Japan in 2016 by Ichijinsha Inc., Tokyo.
Publication rights for this English edition arranged through Kodansha Ltd., Tokyo.

Find more books like this one at www.j-novel.club!

President and Publisher: Samuel Pinansky
Managing Editor: Aimee Zink
QA Manager: Hannah N. Carter
Marketing Manager: Stephanie Hii

ISBN: 978-1-7183-6662-6
Printed in Korea
First Printing: September 2020
10 9 8 7 6 5 4 3 2

Contents

My Next Life All Routes

Jeord Stuart

Third prince of the kingdom, and Katarina's fiancé. Although he looks like a fairy-tale prince with his blonde hair and blue eyes, he secretly harbors a twisted and terrible nature. He once spent his days in boredom, never showing interest in anything, until he met Katarina Claes. His magical element is Fire.

Jeffrey Stuart

The first prince of the kingdom. Most people see him as flippant because of his always-smiling, relaxed demeanor.

Ian Stuart

The second prince of the kingdom.
Very serious, can be difficult to interact with.

Susanna Randall

The second daughter of Marquess Randall.
The first prince's fiancée.

Selena Berg

The oldest daughter of Duke Berg and the second prince's fiancée.

Rufus Brode

A young man working for the Berg family as Selena's personal butler.

Katarina Claes

The only daughter of Duke Claes. Has slanted eyes and angled features, which she thinks make her look like a villainess. After memories of her past life returned, she transformed from a spoiled noble lady to a problem child. Although she often gets ahead of herself, she is honest and straightforward. She has below-average academic and magical ability. Her magical element is Earth.

Luigi Claes

Katarina's father, a Duke and the head of the Claes family who spoils his daughter.

Milidiana Claes

Katarina's mother, and wife of Duke Claes.
Has very angled features like her daughter.

as a Villainess: Lead to Doom!

Nicol Ascart

The son of Royal Chancellor Ascart. An incredibly beautiful and alluring young man who loves his sister, Sophia, deeply. His magical element is Wind.

Keith Claes

Katarina's adopted brother, taken in by the Claes family due to his magical aptitude. Considerably handsome, and seen by others as a chivalrous ladies' man. His magical element is Earth.

Alan Stuart

Jeord's twin brother, and the forth prince of the kingdom. Wildly handsome but also surly and arrogant. Often compares himself to his genius brother, and sulks when he realizes he can't catch up. His magical element is Water.

Sophia Ascart

Daughter of Royal Chancellor Ascart, and Nicol's younger sister. Used to face discrimination due to her white hair and red eyes. A calm and peaceful girl.

Maria Campbell

A commoner, but also a rare "Wielder of Light." The original protagonist of *Fortune Lover* who is very hardworking and loves baking.

Mary Hunt

Fourth daughter of Marquess Hunt, and Alan's fiancée. A lovely and charming girl who's well known as the perfect image of a noble lady.

Raphael Wolt

A young man working at the Magical Ministry. A calm and capable person.

Anne Shelley

Katarina's personal maid who has been with her since childhood.

I, Katarina Claes, was living the good life. My days were pleasant and cozy, and I was usually in a great mood. The reason for this was, of course, because I was now free from the fear of Catastrophic Bad Ends.

On a certain day back when I was eight years old, I accidentally hit my head on a rock, and somehow all the memories of my previous life flooded back into my mind — and it was then that I realized something terrible. Namely, the fact that I was now living in the world of an otome game, and had been reincarnated as the villainess character, Katarina Claes.

To make things worse, Katarina was also the protagonist's rival in four of the game's potential routes, and she had no happy ends of any kind. If the protagonist got a good ending, Katarina would be exiled from the kingdom. If she got a bad ending, Katarina would end up getting killed by the protagonist's love interest. The future that awaited me in this new life as this unfortunate character was nothing but a sea of Catastrophic Bad Ends.

When I realized what was coming, I was thrown into despair. But on the bright side, the plot of the otome game didn't begin until eight years later, when I'd go to the Academy of Magic! I realized that if I worked hard, I might be able to do something about those Bad Ends.

So, ever since that fateful day eight years ago, I worked as hard as I could. I trained fervently in the way of the sword so that I would stand a fighting chance if any of the protagonist's love interests came after me with a weapon. I also practiced my magic as much as possible so that I could use it to survive if I were exiled. To that same end, I prepared to make my living as a humble farmer by eagerly reading up on agriculture.

Eight years passed as I was occupied with all these countermeasures, and before I knew it, I had become fast friends with both the game's four potential love interests and the other rival characters from the game. Although I wasn't sure why we all got along, the other characters and I finally began attending the Academy of Magic last year, entering the main stage of the game.

It was at this academy that we met the game's original protagonist, Maria Campbell. In only a few days, the enchanting Maria was able to capture the attention of my fiancé, Prince Jeord, and my adopted brother, Keith. So impressive was Maria's charm that I lived in fear of her embarking upon the reverse harem route — but despite myself, I also became captivated by the gentle and lovable Maria. While we should have been enemies in the original setting of the game, we instead became close friends.

After this, there was a dangerous episode caused by Sirius, a character that I had completely forgotten about. Fortunately, mainly thanks to my reliable friends, everything was resolved in the end. With that, and some other events along the way, we arrived at the graduation ceremony at the end of that year.

The graduation ceremony was the final event of the otome game — the event in which Maria, the protagonist, would form an eternal connection with someone. Who was it, this person she had chosen for the end of the scenario? Or was it everyone, the reverse harem in which we had all become captivated? I watched on with bated breath. However…

Unexpectedly, the game ended with Maria… not expressing her love for anyone in particular. Instead, we got the "Friendship Ending." As the name suggests, we all simply remained friends. And so Katarina, the villainess and a rival character, did not face any Catastrophic Bad Ends.

Why would we get such an ending, despite Maria's charm…? And then there was the fact that Maria had said the words she would usually say at the end of the game to a love interest, only to me instead. *"So… please, Lady Katarina. Let me stay with you… for now and always."* I couldn't wrap my head around it… Why did Maria say that to *me*?

Well anyway, the game ended safely. I, Katarina Claes, successfully overcame the Catastrophic Bad Ends!

It has been nine years since I regained my memories. Now that those terrible Bad Ends are finally behind me, I can finally live the rest of my peaceful, cozy life.

"The school festival, huh?"

"Yes. The school festival." The one who responded with a familiar faint smile on his face was my fiancé, Jeord Stuart, the third prince of the kingdom.

With his blonde hair and blue eyes, he was the very image of a fairy-tale prince — except for the fact that he was a terrible sadist at heart. If I somehow managed to anger Prince Jeord, even accidentally, I'd be in for some pain. I knew that from experience.

Prince Jeord, however, was seen as a gentle and handsome prince in most circles. He was very popular, especially with noble ladies of our age. The backlash I faced just from being his fiancée was pretty harsh.

Due to his stellar academic performance, Jeord was promoted to the position of Student Council President after we became second-years, and so now he was in charge of all kinds of large-scale projects and duties. That's how we ended up talking about the "school festival." This event was the talk of the academy recently, but…

"I don't remember there being a festival last year, though." I had started at the Academy of Magic last year, and we'd mostly spent our time listening to lectures or attending practical lessons. I didn't remember there being any festive events.

"Yes, of course. School festivals occur once every two years, Katarina. As such, there was no festival last year."

Ohh, once every two years. I guess the Academy of Magic doesn't have yearly festivals like my school in my previous life did. As the Academy of Magic only featured a two-year curriculum, this meant that it was guaranteed to happen once during a student's time at the academy.

But wow, a school festival! Thinking about the ones I'd attended in my previous life, I couldn't help but feel excited. I eagerly asked about the activities and events that would be included.

"Hmm… I suppose there will be outdoor food stalls, and stands where students will be selling their arts and crafts. A student-organized orchestral performance and a play are also on the itinerary… Ah, yes, and there will be a ball held in the evening."

Oh! This is better than I imagined! A true school festival! And students are allowed to put up their own food stalls and art stands? How exciting! Maybe there'll be okonomiyaki and takoyaki too! I hadn't seen any of these foods in this reincarnated life of mine, but maybe they'd be for sale at the festival.

How nostalgic… In my previous life, it was always my goal to have a bite of every single kind of food. Okonomiyaki, takoyaki, yakisoba, chocolate bananas, candied apples, sweet chestnuts, cotton candy... and then...

"...Katarina. Are you listening?"

"...Ah! Yes, sorry." I had completely forgotten about Prince Jeord as my mind was suddenly assaulted by images of food and festival stalls.

"...Well. In any case, I will be busy making the preparations for the festival from now on. For some time, I will no longer be able to have tea with you in this fashion — just the two of us. Please do relax and enjoy yourself today, Katarina." Jeord gave me his usual smile, piercing a piece of food with a fork as he did so. "Here. Have a taste," he said, lifting the pierced bite to my lips.

"Thank you very much!" Just as I was about to chomp down on the morsel, however... the food, fork and all, vanished from before my eyes.

Ah... my food...! My eyes quickly darted over to the person responsible. It was Keith Claes, my adopted brother, who had a grave expression on his face at the moment.

"Prince Jeord. Have you not been ignoring my presence for quite some time now?"

Hmm. Why does it almost seem like Keith is glaring at Jeord?

Jeord, however, simply responded with his ever-present smile fixed in place. "So you say, Keith. But then... consider that I had not invited you in the first place. Why, then, have you invited yourself?"

That was true, Jeord had only invited me. He sent me a note that said: *"I have arranged for a scrumptious spread of food."* But just when I was about to leave, Keith, who had obtained information on this event from some unidentified source, had insisted on coming along with me — which is why we were both in Jeord's quarters. A little strange, considering that Keith hardly had an eye for delicious food in the first place.

11

"But of course, Prince Jeord, I have come along out of sheer worry for my adoptive sister's physical and mental health. It is a most important issue to me."

Huh? So Keith wasn't here for snacks after all? Hmm... So he's that worried about me? What a good brother Keith is, always looking out for his sister. However...

"Surely you jest, Keith. Katarina is merely heading to another room in the same dormitory building — for tea, no less. Are you not being overprotective? It would do you well to give your sister some space, instead of always clinging to her side."

Hmm. Yes, exactly. We are, after all, in the same dormitory. I'm sure I'd be fine even without Keith worrying over me.

With his flaxen hair and blue eyes, Keith was quite handsome. He was also highly capable in his studies, and did well in sports. While I was very proud of my brother, he did tend to worry a little too much. He had become excessively concerned recently, declaring that, *"I simply must be with you when you meet with Prince Jeord, Big Sister."*

I suppose it was somewhat dangerous in the past — in one of the Catastrophic Bad Ends, Jeord could have exiled me, or even drawn his blade upon me if I ever made a terrible mistake... but that was no longer a concern. With the events of *Fortune Lover* now over, along with the fact that we had achieved the "Friendship Ending," this danger was now effectively over.

As I continued pondering about this, the two of them continued their own little conversation, now apparently facing each other with visible smiles.

"But you see, if her destination is this particular room, then I must be present as well. After all, it is simply too dangerous for my adoptive sister to be in this place by herself."

"Whatever would you mean to imply, Keith?"

"Perhaps you should look within yourself for the answer to that question, Prince Jeord."

...*Hmm.* I could no longer follow their conversation. As Jeord and Keith continued their seemingly friendly talk, full of smiles, I found myself isolated once more. The two of them were quite fond of doing this — they would get lost in conversation, in that little world of theirs, and soon enough there would be nothing for me to add.

I've known them both for a long time. It's nice to see them get along so well! I decided to just quietly help myself to the food on the table. *Ooooh. These treats are impressively delicious. I should have everyone else try them too.*

With that, my fiancé and brother, now fully engrossed in their own conversation, said little about me helping myself to the delicious food. Which was perfectly fine with me.

Shortly after I heard about the school festival from Jeord, preparations for the event began in full force. In the Academy of Magic, students were separated by year — and although the lecture halls looked like the classrooms I was used to, the size of a single class was simply immense. So it didn't seem like each individual class would be putting up an attraction of their own, which was how it had been in my previous life. Instead, students would form groups between friends or relatives and ask for permission to put up attractions.

Alright then! I should apply to, or maybe even make my own group to sell the crops I've worked so hard on! At least, that was what I thought... But Jeord, Keith, and to my surprise, even Alan all strongly opposed the idea. I suggested that I could hand them out for free, but that idea was rejected too. Apparently, the sale of crops didn't suit the "image" of the Academy of Magic.

My hard-earned crops, "unsuitable"? Ever since coming to the academy, I hadn't been able to use up as many vegetables as I did back home, so I had a lot left over. *I thought that this would be a good opportunity to sell off that stock... What a bummer.*

I really was sad about it! However, the always angelic Maria quickly said to me: "Well then, Lady Katarina... if I may suggest, perhaps I could use the vegetables you have so lovingly cultivated in my baked goods?"

Ah, Maria is so sweet. I'd consider it an honor if my vegetables were used in her treats. After all, Maria's baked goods were really something else — in fact, I felt like she was on the same level as a professional patissier. Her treats were amazing.

So now, there wouldn't be an issue with using up my vegetables. It was simple, then — Maria would make treats with the crops I'd grown, and we would simply sell those products at our stand instead. Although concerns were raised about such food not being very popular in a noble-dominated academy like this one, I was passionate about the idea. When I said "Well, it's either that or my crops," I quickly received permission for the venture. *Well done, Katarina Claes.*

Since I was the one who brought up this entire idea in the first place, I decided to help my friends in the council as much as I could. Members of the council were saddled with a lot of work in preparation for the festival, and could use whatever help they could get.

The student body had apparently strongly requested that the student council put on a play of some sort. I supposed that made sense, considering the number of beautiful people on the council in general — it went without saying that they each had their fair share of fans.

The council agreed to honor this request from the students. Although my friends tried to insist on me joining the performance, I repeatedly rejected their offers. After all, I had only played the roles of inanimate objects like trees and rocks during school performances in my previous life. A play where all the actors had lines would simply be too much for someone like me.

Just to be sure, I asked my friends if they were in need of a rock, or perhaps even a tree. But they responded incredulously, "Are such roles even needed...?" *What a shame...! Those were roles that I perfected in my previous life!*

However, I did feel a little bad about simply sitting in the council chambers, snacking and not doing anything to help out. So I decided to help my friends with any backstage work they needed done.

Leave it to me if there are any scenes where throwing an object is required! After all, I was particularly confident in my throwing skills after practicing for long hours with my projectile snakes. *Huh? There's no scenes that need projectiles...? That's too bad.*

Between helping Maria with her vegetable-based baked goods and assisting my friends with the production of their play, the days passed by quickly. Before I knew it, the day of the school festival arrived.

With the conclusion of Student Council President Jeord's address, along with the almost deafening squeals and sighs of the noble ladies in the crowd, the school festival was now officially underway. Even the usually more reserved noble ladies in the student body were visibly excited today, and I was no exception.

15

Festivals were always fun for me in my previous life, and this was the first festival I'd attend in this new one! Since I was the daughter of a duke, I had been to many balls and parties, but a festival was something else altogether. I had never been to one in this world.

And so, while I was already delighted at having overcome the Catastrophic Bad Ends, I was especially excited and in good spirits today — perhaps the happiest I had ever been since coming to the academy... or even since the start of this new life. In fact, I had to be careful to restrain myself from skipping and humming a tune.

Actually, I had been so excited that I had started dancing alone in my room last night, much to Anne's chagrin. It would seem that it was unbecoming for a noble lady to skip along or hum a tune. These were simply not things a lady should do in front of others, or so I was told. Being a noble lady kind of sucked.

There was also the fact that guardians and parents would be attending the school festival too. My mother, however, apparently claimed that... "Alas, it would be too embarrassing. I would greatly prefer to abstain from this event." *Hmm. Given how resolute Mother is at home, why would she be ashamed outside of it? A lion at home, a mouse abroad...*

I asked Anne for her opinion, and she said, "Young miss, if I may say so... I assume that the madam is not embarrassed... of herself," all while regarding me with a disappointed gaze.

Hmm? What's that supposed to mean? In the end, I didn't quite understand.

Even so, my father seemed to be very interested in showing up at the school festival, and given the lovey-dovey couple that they were, the possibility of both of them showing up was somewhat high.

If Mother did appear on the academy grounds and saw me skipping along, humming a tune… I dreaded to even think about how many hours she would spend lecturing me. Yes, I'd have to be careful.

Although I continued to suppress my urge to skip and hum tunes, I ended up fidgeting noticeably instead, and I could hardly contain the excitement in my voice. The group of girls near me noticed, and one of them kindly asked, "Lady Katarina, are you perhaps unwell?"

"Ah, not at all! It's nothing! In fact, I'm just fidgeting from excitement!" I responded honestly. The girls smiled in response, apparently sharing my feelings.

My classmates are all so nice to me. Under normal circumstances, I would have followed around the members of the student council. But today, they were all assigned to specific spots on the grounds and couldn't just drop their duties to hang out with me, so I found myself exploring the festival with my other friends and classmates.

My friends on the council had seemed sad at this turn of events, saying things like:

"To think that I would be unable to accompany you during the festival…"

"If I had known, I would never have taken on this role…"

"Ah, my chance to be with Lady Katarina during the one festival in our time…"

In an effort to cheer up my ailing friends, I decided to buy a bunch of snacks and visit each of them in turn. Although they were sad that they couldn't spend our one academy festival with me, they'd definitely cheer up once I brought them some delicious food!

Alright! Takoyaki, yakisoba, okonomiyaki… here I come! I thought as I rushed towards the student stands. Unfortunately…

Th-This is… the stands at the festival are…! I stood there, alone and disappointed. *This wasn't what I'd expected from festival stands at all…*

They should be kinda janky, run by old men wearing greasy clothing or yankee-like young guys calling out "Hey, wanna buy some?" or something like that…

Instead, I was faced with beautifully-constructed, chic structures. Standing inside them were uniformed young men who were formally thanking people for visiting their humble establishments. *THESE are the food stands at the academy? Even if this IS the Academy of Magic… I can't accept this, I simply can't!*

However, the biggest shock was yet to come… These "food stands" were only selling sandwiches and croissants! Yes, these were the only foods on sale at this so-called "school festival" at the Academy of Magic. Chic and fancy as they may be, sandwiches and croissants were hardly satisfying.

No matter how hard I looked, I couldn't find any okonomiyaki, yakisoba, or takoyaki. In fact, all these stands sold more or less the same thing — the sort of simple pastries, hors d'oeuvres, or haute cuisine that nobles would have at their tea-parties…

I'd already planned for this stomach of mine to be filled with okonomiyaki… takoyaki… yakisoba. I had planned for this! My dessert was going to be a chocolate banana! And cotton candy! And yet… and yet! In almost an instant, my excitement and good spirits had completely disappeared. I was a husk of my former self.

The classmates who were with me were visibly alarmed.

"L-Lady Katarina! Are you quite alright?"

"Whatever has happened? You were so cheerful up until a moment ago!"

"Does your stomach hurt, Lady Katarina?"

"No, perhaps she is hungry? I shall purchase something for her..."

I had left my stomach empty on purpose, hoping to allow for the joys of my previous life to fill me up. I had been anticipating this meal... and yet, now I was unable to eat it! I was filled with a deep sense of loss.

"Haa... haa..." my classmate panted as she returned. "L-Lady Katarina. I h-have... brought you something to eat. Please, have some of this. I pray that you will be in good spirits again soon..." She presented me with what appeared to be a sandwich on an elaborately decorated plate.

My classmates have apparently assumed that I was sad because I hadn't had enough to eat. ...*Hm? What exactly do they think of me, then?*

I had honestly already lost my appetite, having realized that I was unable to have my favorite okonomiyaki and yakisoba. But my kind classmate had gone through the trouble of getting this sandwich for me. With a simple "thank you," I brought the sandwich to my mouth.

And then... *This...! THIS TASTE!* "Wh-What is this?! This is completely different from the sandwiches I usually have! What is this fluffiness, this softness of the bread? This incredibly delicious jam? Tell me at once! Where exactly is this bread from?!"

I was surprised — no, *overwhelmed* — by the delicious force of the sandwich in my mouth. Before I could restrain myself, my face was already uncomfortably close to my kind classmate's, my nostrils flaring in excitement. The other students collectively withdrew, before answering stutteringly.

19

"...Y-Yes. Of course, Lady Katarina... the school festival of the Academy of Magic is quite the significant affair. It usually attracts stands from various famous shops and establishments across the land, who send samples of their newest work to the festival to be sold. As such, the food here is usually most delicious... In fact, there are some who call it the 'Festival of Gourmet Food.' I have heard that there are many people who show up at the festival just to have a taste of this particular store's products..."

What?! How could this be! I never knew that the food stands could be this... impressive, this incredible...! While it was unfortunate that they didn't have my favorite okonomiyaki and other festival foods, now that I had a closer look... the offerings of these stands did look really good.

And then there was the matter of famous shops and establishments selling their newest products at the festival... *This is a rare opportunity. I can't miss this.* With those thoughts in mind, there was no way I could keep feeling sad. *I have to eat! Eat! EAT! EAT ALL OF IT!*

"Alright! Everyone, let's go! We shall tour the stands from this starting point here!" With my loud declaration, I led my classmates on, eager to start my gourmet crusade.

They all merely smiled and said things like, "It was as I thought... Lady Katarina was simply hungry," and "I am glad that she's cheered up once more." Now that anticipation was back in my bones, I needed to only do one thing — tour and chomp down on the offerings of any stand that caught my eye.

Ah, this bread... this sandwich. It was simply too delicious. Oh...? What about this potato salad here...? It looks, just as good, I think.

"…Um, Lady Katarina."

Ooooh! I have never seen anything quite like that dessert over there. It must be a new product…! I simply have to taste it.

"…Lady Katarina."

Ah, what about this cake over here? It looks tasty as well. Or that pudding there…

"Excuse me, Lady Katarina!"

"Eh, ah, yes. Sorry. Did you need something?"

How dangerous… that was close. My attention had been completely commandeered by the offerings of the festival stands.

"…Um, well. Did you not have plans to meet with each member of the student council today, Lady Katarina…?"

"Oh, yes. That's right."

"If you still do intend to make your rounds, Lady Katarina, we really do need to be going soon… for fear of you running out of time, you see…" my classmate warned, her brows furrowed with worry.

"Huh…?!" I confirmed the time in a panic, only to realize that I'd already spent a lot of time at the food stands. "Wh-What! How could it be this time already?"

I had been completely charmed by the allure of these delicious foods. If my classmates hadn't warned me, I probably would have stayed here and continued to eat until the festival ended. *That was close… The temptation of scrumptious food is a terrifying thing.*

Finally back to my senses, I went and purchased a large amount of food and gifts for my friends on the council, as well as an equally large amount for myself. Then, with the classmates who had brought me back to my senses, we rushed off to where the student council members were stationed.

First, we headed for the person who was closest to us. We found ourselves in an exhibition space showcasing the history of the kingdom, as well as research on various magical theories.

In my previous life, hardly anyone would be found at an academic exhibit like this. But this was the Academy of Magic, and there were a fair number of students and their parents eagerly looking at the displays. I thought their never-ending thirst for knowledge was commendable... but I'd definitely fall asleep after reading just a few lines.

Standing at this exhibition were my adopted brother Keith and my friend Mary, the daughter of Marquess Hunt. They were both hard at work, smiling and greeting the attendees.

Like me, Mary was also the fiancée to a prince. She was engaged to Prince Alan Stuart, who was Jeord's twin brother. But although we were both engaged to princes and hence were of similar social standing, unlike me, Mary was extremely capable and high-spec.

Mary's hair was a deep shade of burnt sienna, and her eyes were the same color. She did very well in school, but was also said to have the grace of a fairy when she danced. She was the very image of what a refined, noble lady should aspire to be.

Many noble ladies looked up to the royal princes, of course, and while they would often criticize me for being "unable to match Prince Jeord at all," they had nothing but praise for Mary, often saying that she was "most suitable for Prince Alan."

That very same perfect noble lady, however, now seemed a little tired from the sheer number of visitors she was greeting... maybe even a little out of it? Perhaps she was hungry? After all, it was already past noon. Judging by the look of things, it wouldn't be surprising if she hadn't had a chance to have lunch.

The more I thought about Mary's plight, the more I felt guilty for standing outside at the stands, eating as much as I could. *Alright, then! I'll hand over one of the special sandwiches that I purchased for myself. A new recipe, from what I heard.*

With those thoughts in mind, I held the bag of sandwiches in my hands, calling out to Mary as I approached. "Mary! I brought something for you."

"Lady Katarina!" Mary gave me a vibrant smile upon noticing my approach, as if she wasn't tired at all.

As I expected, she's hungry. "I'm sorry for coming so late, Mary! Here, try this… I heard this sandwich is a new recipe!"

"I am delighted that you have decided to come by, Lady Katarina. I was worried… since you hadn't returned from the stands after quite some time…"

"Ah… yes. Sorry about that." We had passed by this space on our way to the stands, and had seen Mary briefly then. I'd told her that we were just going to have a look… and ended up being gone for a long time. *Of course she'd be worried. I'm so sorry, Mary!*

"Big Sister… if I had to guess, you simply lost track of time, sampling one new dish or another, no?" Keith said, sighing as he did so.

Brothers know best. I now see that our family bond of more than eight years has gifted him with incredible insight. At the very least, Keith seemed to know a lot about his sister.

"…I'm sorry." I bowed my head once more to the worried Mary and Keith.

"Think nothing of it, Lady Katarina. I am only glad that you are safe," Mary said, smiling gently.

Keith, on the other hand… "Really, Big Sister. Are you not being a little too careless? You do have a habit of getting into trouble. Please be aware of that… and be more careful," he said with a strict look about him.

For some reason, it seemed like Keith was taking after Mother more and more as the years went by. If this went on, there would eventually come a day where he would spend hours lecturing me, just as Mother would. Two mothers… would I be able to endure such a thing?

"Lady Katarina, the crowds are thinning as we speak. We were just thinking of having a short rest soon, perhaps, and maybe having something to eat. I am most grateful for the food you have brought us. Would you like to eat together with us?" Mary, having made a complete recovery, was now looking out for me instead.

"R-Really?!" Honestly, I did feel a bit of regret for handing out that limited, new-recipe sandwich. I wanted to try it too.

"Big Sister… have you not already had quite a lot to eat? You wish to eat some more?" Keith inquired, looking at me with an exasperated expression. The classmates who had followed me to the stands seemed equally surprised.

Oh no… if I keep gorging myself like this, everyone will think I'm a total pig. But that's not true! I'm normal! It's just that noble ladies eat too little. Plus, these dresses are way too tight. Maybe they just can't eat as much as they want to because they're bound up in them.

I had asked for my own dress to be loosened, all for the sake of gorging myself at the stands today. My maid Anne wasn't too thrilled about the prospect, and had protested vehemently. *"Young miss, why would you want to loosen such a spectacular dress…?"* she'd said. But I threatened to show up in my farming overalls if it wasn't done, and she eventually gave in to my request.

That's why I can eat more than everyone else! I'm definitely not a pig!

But… I guess I should only have a little bit… So I amended my earlier outburst. "…Yes, Mary. Just a little."

And so, Mary, Keith, and I ended up sitting at a resting space at the venue, where tea was served and sandwiches eaten. I asked the classmates with me to join us for tea, but they politely declined. "We are already quite full, Lady Katarina. We shall go have a look at the exhibits instead."

Don't you understand, my dear classmates? All you have to do is to loosen your dresses!

"Wow… it does look delicious!" The sandwich was quite different from the ones I had before.

"Why yes, it does look most appetizing indeed. Thank you very much, Lady Katarina," Mary said, smiling faintly at me as I started drooling at the sight of the sandwich.

"Big Sister… did you not already have quite a lot to eat? Please eat in moderation, or you'll get a stomach ache," Keith said. He really did understand his sister…

"…Yes, I understand." *But I already loosened my dress in advance! There should be no problems!* With that in mind, I reached for a piece of the sandwich and popped it into my mouth.

Ah… yummy! The first store's sandwich was more of a snack food, with the jam at its center. But this one was filled with fresh lettuce and crispy, fried bacon. It felt more like a main course than a snack. There were so many different kinds of sandwiches!

Ah… that one over there with the potato salad in it looks good too. And then there's this one here, with bits of egg in the center… Hmm. I was at a loss — I wanted to sample all the different kinds!

Oh, I know! "Hey, Keith… could I split the sandwiches with you? I'll have half."

"…Sure. I thought you might say that, Big Sister."

"Hooray!"

Although the portion sizes of food in this world were relatively small, there was a large variety available. I suppose that was more of a cultural feature amongst nobles, as opposed to the rest of the world at large — but even so, there really was an impressive variety of foods. I always wanted to eat whatever was rare or caught my attention.

In my previous life, my mother had taught me to leave both my plates and chopsticks clean, and her teachings remained alive and well in my heart to this day. But as a result, I often ended up eating too much and getting stomach aches.

When he saw this, Keith would always say: *"If you would like to try a bit of everything, Big Sister, how about you split half of it with me? I will finish the other half for you."* So while I couldn't exactly do it openly in a public space, I often sneakily split my meals in half back at Claes Manor. Keith finished the rest, of course.

Since Keith said he was fine with it, I took the potato salad sandwich in my hands, splitting it into two equal halves to the best of my ability. I held out one half to Keith's lips. "Here you go, Keith! Try some."

Under normal circumstances, Keith would usually eat anything I offered him without a second thought. But today, his expression was strangely blank — and also frozen. I wondered if something was wrong.

"Is something the matter, Keith?"

"A-Ah… well. Big Sister… could we perhaps not do this in public, and in full view of others?"

"Others? But this isn't really a public venue. Didn't you just say it was fine just moments ago?"

"Well… I didn't mean it in this particular way… that…"

Hmm. Keith is acting suspiciously.

"Hmm? So the two of you always do this, as long as you are not in a public space…?" For some reason, Mary had the most dazzling smile on her face as she posed her question.

"Ah, right. When I have something that I want to taste, but can't finish it all, I usually split half of it and give it to Keith."

"Is that right? And so, Lady Katarina… do you mean to say that this half portion is always fed to Master Keith's lips… with your hands?"

"Of course. It wasn't like that at first, but Keith asked me to feed him that way whenever we split food a while ago, so now I always do."

It was exactly so. Although we had split food for as long as I could remember, Keith had requested that I feed him the split half by hand. *I wonder why he asked for that? Is it because it's annoying to have to reach for the portion himself?* I didn't really understand why — if anything, this was really a social faux pas when it came to dining etiquette, especially for Keith.

Keith rarely made requests of me though, so I decided to oblige, and ended up feeding him in this way ever since. Upon hearing my explanation, Mary's smile became deeper, and more… intense. *Hmm? What is this tension, in the air?*

"…Master Keith. Did you not agree that you would not abuse your position as a family member, and keep her all to yourself? You did, did you not?"

"N-No… Nothing of the sort! This is hardly anything special…! It's not as if I would lay my hands on her in any uncouth ways, unlike Prince Jeord!"

"Please do not bring Prince Jeord into this conversation, or use him as a point of reference. He is abnormal! I had thought that you were far too awkward, not even trying to hold hands… A miscalculation on my part."

"Lady Mary, you know I can hear you despite your muffled whispers. What a thing to say! This is the height of rudeness! Do you not also abuse the fact that you're a woman? You engage in excessive bodily contact — hugging, touching… Is that not true?"

"Oh my. Abuse, Master Keith? How equally rude of you. It is most normal for girls to hug and touch each other, is it not? And then eventually… slowly… even share a bath together…"

"I must disagree, Lady Mary. What you just said cannot possibly be construed as normal."

"Alas, Master Keith. Does that not say more about you and your perspective instead?"

What's going on? For some reason, the act of me splitting my food seemed to put quite the fire under these two. They were now locked in an intensely escalating conversation, each sentence more passionate than the last.

I knew that Keith and Jeord got along well, but apparently Keith and Mary did too! The way they talked without hesitation, I couldn't see anything but two people who truly empathized with each other.

…*Huh?! Could it be?* The person who Keith liked… The reason for him turning down wave after wave of suitors… I'd assumed all this time that it was the original protagonist of *Fortune Lover*, Maria. *But could it be? Mary?*

Mary was very unlike how she'd been portrayed in the game. She wasn't interested in Alan, so could it be that she had feelings for Keith? A potential love interest and a rival character from another route... This would have been an impossible match-up in the game. But the current reality was after the events of *Fortune Lover* had already ended. The impossible could very well be possible.

My woman's intuition is terrifying indeed... I continued looking at the two, still passionately engaged in conversation. Keith had no fiancée, and Mary was engaged to the fourth prince of the kingdom, Alan. Although the two weren't married yet, Alan seemed to value Mary greatly. In fact, the way that he had been following Mary around recently... he almost looked like an underling. *Hmm. Wait, no. More like a knight protecting his princess.*

This was a forbidden love. One that cannot be easily permitted or forgiven. *"O Keith, Keith! Wherefore art thou Keith?" "Ah, Mary!"* The scenes from a particularly famous romantic tragedy rose up from the depths of my mind... with Keith and Mary as the main cast. *Ahh, how sad!*

I looked at the two intensely before declaring my intent. "Keith... Mary. Should the time ever come to pass, I will definitely side with you both, don't you worry! Even if any mistakes are made... I will not allow this to become a romantic tragedy, like Romeo and the rest!"

The two immediately went silent upon witnessing my passionate gaze. It was as if the intense conversation they were having had never occurred in the first place.

"Big Sister... I don't quite know what you're thinking in that head of yours — but I am very sure that whatever conclusion you've arrived at, it is most mistaken."

Huh? I was wrong? B-But my woman's intuition...

"I would have to agree as well, Lady Katarina. I vehemently reject such a conclusion," Mary said in a firm, yet calm voice.

But... I still hadn't asked! I couldn't be sure! Maybe I should be more specific, just to be sure...

"...Um. Then... the love between Keith and Mary...?"

"You are most mistaken," the two of them declared, not allowing me to finish my sentence.

...Is that so? For a while after, both Keith and Mary looked at me with disappointed gazes. *Why?*

The two of them then asked me who "Romeo" was. I suppose they were itching to know. "A main character in a romantic tragedy," I answered, before leaving the resting area behind.

After meeting up with my classmates who were touring the exhibits, we continued our journey. This time we headed towards the stage area where plays and performances were taking place. It resembled the school gymnasium in my previous life; a stage would be set up there, and the band or drama club would use it for their performances. Well, in this case, I would say that it was more like a real theatre — a well-constructed, respectable building.

Sophia was waiting for me there... or at least, she should have been. We arrived just when a performance had ended, and the audience was currently filing away. I looked near the entrances and exits of the stage, but couldn't find anyone.

Hmm? Is it break-time, maybe? I decided to ask a nearby first-year about it.

"Ah, Lady Ascart? She had a visitor, I believe? It got a little... out of hand, so she headed to the backstage area..."

A visitor? Out of hand? I didn't understand what that was supposed to mean, but I figured that all I could do was go backstage and see for myself.

"Ah, Lady Katarina. I am glad that you have come..." Greeting me was a beautiful girl with hair like strands of white silk and a pair of ruby-red eyes. Sophia was a close friend of mine on the student council, and the daughter of Count Ascart.

Standing behind her was her elder brother Nicol, with his jet-black hair and eyes — the Alluring Count. I was the only one who referred to him that way, though. As usual, his charm aura was in full bloom.

"It is good to see you, Katarina," he said with that familiar seductive smile. While Nicol was usually stoic and expressionless, these occasional smiles of his were deadly weapons. That was how charming he was. In these past few years, the power of his smile had only increased exponentially, and even a long-time friend of Nicol's such as myself couldn't help but blush in response.

"...A-Ah. Yes. You as well, Master Nicol." I mustered up all of the Nicol Resistance I had within myself, and somehow managed to respond somewhat normally.

Maybe it was because I hadn't seen Nicol for quite some time, but it was almost like he was... sparkling. No matter how long I had known him, a single lapse in my attention was enough for my mind to completely blank out. But more importantly...

"Why are you hiding in the backstage area, Sophia? Since you're both here, wouldn't you draw a lot of people in if you were standing out front instead?"

Come to think of it, Jeord had even said that was the whole point. The members of the student council were each positioned at their assigned spots precisely because they were popular and they'd attract people to those particular locations. In other words... the members of the student council were like mascots — no, beacons in charge of attracting students to their areas.

Given that it wasn't even break time, it was a waste for them both to hide in the back like this. After all, the Ascart siblings were both impossibly beautiful. They were almost like living dolls. Nicol, in particular, seemed to appeal to both men and women — the Alluring Count and his indiscriminating aura of oppressive charm.

Although Nicol had graduated last year, and as such was no longer a student of the Academy of Magic, he was still an ex-council member, and I assumed that he was here to help with the event. I posed my question to Sophia, and she responded with a troubled expression.

"In truth… I had assumed that many students would come to this venue if Big Brother stood at the entrance, too… and so I had him stand there…"

Ah, so that's what they were doing. Huh? Then why are they here right now? "Well then… why hide in the backstage area now?"

"You see, Lady Katarina… it was indeed true, many students were attracted to our allocated area, but… they became much like how all of you are right now."

I followed Sophia's gaze to my other classmates, who were currently rooted to the ground and staring at Nicol fixedly, their faces beet red. *M-My friends…*

"Everyone just kept staring at him, to the point where the performers were upset! No one was paying any attention to them… And so we were told to go somewhere where no one would see us…" Sophia said, her sad gaze locking onto mine.

…I see. I guess there was no choice… After all, they'd just draw attention away from the actual event if they stayed out there. It was impossible to tell the Alluring Count not to stand out. His very presence filled the air around him with glamorous, radiant sparkles.

I placed a hand on Sophia's sadly slumped shoulders and gave her a few good pats. "Don't worry, Sophia! I brought you a little something from the stands. I'm sure this treat will cheer you right up!"

"Thank you very much, Lady Katarina…" Sophia said, smiling faintly. As always, upon seeing the Alluring Count's sister smiling like that, even a woman like me felt my heart skip a beat.

I handed Sophia and Nicol some fluffy chocolate pastries that were something between bread and cake in terms of consistency. Surely, filling their bellies with this tasty treat would cheer them up.

"Come to think of it, Lady Katarina… you ended up not participating in the student council play," Sophia said, as if suddenly remembering this fact. She spoke as she nibbled on the treat, her cheeks puffed out like a little squirrel. She was simply too adorable — before I knew it, I found myself wanting to rub her rosy cheeks.

Mother and Anne, however, always seemed to snap angrily at me whenever I'd stuffed my cheeks full of snacks. *"Don't stuff your food into your cheeks like that!"* they would say. I wonder what the difference between Sophia and me was?

"Ah, that. Well, I'm not really a member of the council after all, and I don't really have any acting talent." While it was true that I had blended in with the rest of the council for the past year, to the point where even the new first-years thought I was a member, participating in a performance was another thing altogether. When it came to something like this, I was an outsider.

And anyway, the script for the play was much like the story of Cinderella that I had read in my previous life. There was no way I'd have the confidence to play any role in such a glittering, glamorous drama. There weren't any roles for rocks and trees. Though since I was always in the council chambers, I had made it a point to assist my friends behind the scenes — cleaning up tools, helping with props, and whatnot.

"Ah... I had hoped that I would see you on stage, Lady Katarina..." Sophia said, her shoulders slumping again in disappointment.

Even Nicol, who was standing beside her, looked equally disappointed. "...I see. So Katarina will not be performing..." he said, a hint of regret in his voice.

Huh? Why are they so down? Yet even those somewhat pained expressions of theirs were attractive in their own way. My classmates, who were still standing behind me, now had their eyes unfocused, as if in a daze... *You doing okay over there, friends?*

Maybe Nicol and Sophia were only expressing such sorrow because I was a childhood friend of theirs. It's not like I was as attractive as the other members of the council. I couldn't imagine a council play needing someone like me, with my villainess face. Instead...

"But wouldn't it make more sense for you to star in a performance, Master Nicol? After all, you never did anything like that during your school festival. How about starring in a guest role in a short performance?"

While the Alluring Count Nicol Ascart did have his own school festival when he was a first-year, the council was overloaded with work then, and was too busy to put on any kind of performance. That was what a second-year on the council had told me.

As for the work the council had been suddenly loaded with... Well, from what I was told, it was dealing with everyone who had been charmed by the Count's alluring aura.

"...Sadly, Katarina, I am incapable of acting," Nicol replied after a thoughtful pause.

"…Incapable, Master Nicol?"

"Hmm… I do think so, Lady Katarina… Big Brother would be a little troubled if he had to act." Sophia was the one to respond to my inquiry. "Although he is an amazing person — and I would say this even if he were not my own brother — he unfortunately finds it difficult to control what emotions he shows outwardly. It is quite the flaw…"

"Oh, yeah… That's right…" Although Nicol's gamut of emotions had increased recently, from him smiling to even showing expressions of disappointment, those occurrences were spontaneous. Apparently, Nicol wasn't able to smile on command. Ever since coming to the academy, I'd noticed that while he did portray a range of emotions when he was with me and my friends, he was completely stoic in any other location and setting.

And so, the discussion shifted to urging Nicol to practice his smiling so that he could smile in other situations as well.

"Well then, Master Nicol. Please try to smile!" I said.

"I will," Nicol responded, and gave his best. And then, the all-too-familiar alluring smile that I had seen all these years… was nowhere to be found. No matter how much I waited, I was only met with a slight twitch at the side of Nicol's lips.

In the end, I had to resign myself to the fact that Nicol was incapable of smiling on purpose… or, at the very least, was unable to control his expressions easily. *What a shocking development! The omnipotent Nicol's one and only flaw…*

It was then that I realized — wouldn't it be hard for him, as a noble, to not be able to smile when needed? Though in Nicol's case, I supposed his stoic expression was more than enough to charm people of all genders, given his Alluring Aura. It would probably work out, in his case.

I see... so this is what the gods of the world had in mind for Nicol. In exchange for his alluring aura and charms, he is unable to smile freely. For some reason, I was convinced that this theory was correct.

Hmm. With that in mind, I suppose having to act would be pretty hard for him. But of course, there's always the option of playing the role of a rock, or perhaps a tree...

"Ah... but if it is you, Lady Katarina, a smile would surely come across Big Brother's face," Sophia said, as if suddenly coming up with a fabulous idea.

But I disagreed. "In that case, wouldn't it make more sense for his practice partner to be you, Sophia?"

After all, Nicol loved his little sister very much. He had followed closely behind her ever since they were children. Even after graduating from the academy, he would still come by to visit, sneakily checking on his sister out of worry. Well, considering that Sophia was just as beautiful (naturally, being related to Nicol), I could understand why he worried about her so much.

"Alas... I do not have the strength. The one who can draw out Big Brother's smile is you alone, Lady Katarina."

"Ah, no, but then I wouldn't be able to either—"

"No, that is not true, Lady Katarina!" Sophia insisted. "Ah! How about we have Big Brother say some lines from the play right now? You can be the actress opposite him. Surely he will say these lines with a smile."

For some reason, Sophia had suddenly cheered up, and declared that she was insufficient for the role. No matter how much I tried to escape from the situation, she simply insisted that I participate, her eyes sparkling with expectation as she told her brother the lines from the play.

Seeing how happy Sophia was, I relented. *If it's to make Sophia that happy, I guess it's alright,* I thought. Nicol did love his sister, and Sophia also admired her brother greatly. I supposed she simply wanted to see her brother finally get a good grasp on acting.

Having me as Nicol's partner in this exercise was, of course, to keep the gazes of the audience on the Alluring Count himself. *Alright, then! I shall try my very best to be the partner of the Count, all of the sake of the darling Sophia.*

The scene that she had requested of Nicol was one from the climax of the play — the main romantic scene. To be specific, it was the scene where the prince lovingly strokes the hair of the girl he loves, smiling gently. He would then whisper sweet nothings into her ear and hold her tight.

The only line that the partner actress had in this scene was "Me too, Prince…" Even I, who only had experience playing rocks and trees, wouldn't have a problem with such a short line. *Well then, bring it on! I shall give it my all for Sophia's sake.*

"Okay, please go ahead, Master Nicol!" I said, standing before Nicol and drawing myself up to my full height dauntingly.

Sophia quickly whispered, "Lady Katarina… psst! The way you are standing…!"

Ah, silly me. I have to stand more like… a princess would. I brought my feet closer together from my previously wide stance.

With all the preparations complete, Nicol slowly approached. I could see traces of nervousness on his face. We weren't even standing on an actual stage, and the only people watching were Sophia and my starstruck classmates. *Does Nicol dislike acting this much?*

"…Sophia. I…"

"No, Big Brother. You must try. After all, you have already graduated from the academy, and we are at a clear disadvantage! We have to seize the opportunity and approach at this crucial moment!"

Nicol and Sophia seemed to be whispering about something. As expected, it would seem that Nicol was not very keen on going through with this. However, Sophia was being somewhat insistent, given that she had so much sisterly love for Nicol.

In the end, unable to deny his lovable sister's request, Nicol stood before me once more. I could see the resolve on his face. "Are you ready, Katarina?"

"Yes. I shall do my best to be your partner in this endeavor, Master Nicol, for Sophia's sake! You can count on me." Although it was the first time I had played a human, this wasn't a real stage, and was only a one-off. *I shall strive to be the best actress I can be, and overcome this challenge!*

"Is that so…? Thank you." Nicol's alluring smile showed itself once more.

Ugh, this is bad. My face was already bright red thanks to Nicol's overflowing charm. *Endure it, actress Katarina Claes!*

As I continued my best attempts at enduring the experience, Nicol ran his fingers through my long hair, gently and slowly. I could feel my heartbeat increasing as his long, beautiful fingers ran smoothly through my hair. His charm was simply too much to handle. If this went on I would lose my mind too, just like my unfortunate classmates behind me. I was already close to my limit.

With his stunning smile, Nicol delivered his line from the play: "I love you."

I could feel the strength leave my legs upon hearing his sweet, seductive voice. But I had developed a respectably high amount of Nicol Resistance, having known him all these years, so I managed to struggle out my line.

"…M-Me… too. Master Nicol." Upon hearing my line, however, Nicol's smile… froze.

Huh? Why? AH! I delivered my lines wrong! I, Katarina Claes, who had been so unfortunately swayed by the charming wiles of the Alluring Count, had ended up calling the Prince "Master Nicol" instead. *H-How could I have messed up such a short, simple line... Nicol must be frozen in place, stunned at my incompetence.*

"Um... Master Nicol..." Before I could finish my apology of "I'm so sorry for messing up!" — I realized that I was in Nicol's arms.

Ah... I guess he wants to continue, in spite of my mistake. Hmm. But... the way he's holding me is more... passionate, than I expected. Stronger than I expected. More importantly, what's this pleasant smell, now that I'm so close?

This... this is bad. I could feel my mind slipping into emptiness, taken by the alluring aura. With my consciousness somewhat impaired, I could hear Nicol whisper something in my ear. Strangely, he sounded pained.

"...Katarina. Even if you belong to someone else... I... will certainly..."

Huh? Is that one of the lines? I wondered briefly. The sweet, charming words whispered into my ears soon took effect, and I promptly stopped thinking.

From somewhere far away, I felt like I could hear Sophia's voice. "You did it, Big Brother!"

...ACK! Where is this? Where am I? When I regained some semblance of consciousness, we were already a considerable distance away from Sophia and Nicol.

Honestly, I didn't have any memory of saying goodbye to them. In fact, I could hardly remember anything from after I wrongly delivered my line. It would appear that I had lost my memories due to the incredible charm of the Alluring Count.

In addition, the friends and classmates who were with me claimed that they remembered nothing of the meeting at all — their memories were apparently blank, and the last thing they could recall was Nicol's smile. *The Alluring Count is truly fearsome...*

And with that, our little group was finally aware and conscious once more. Our next destination was a space dedicated to displaying and selling things made by the academy students. Gathered here were various handicrafts — embroidery, art pieces, and even some products and art created by the Magical Ministry's research facility on the campus.

Maria was here, with her homemade baked goods on sale. My classmates wanted to look at the embroidery, so we parted ways and I headed over to her. With her blonde hair and clear, blue eyes, I would say that Maria was the most, if not at least second most beautiful girl in the academy. It didn't take long for me to find her. Although it was quite different from Nicol's oppressive force, the charming Maria easily drew many pairs of eyes to her.

"Maria!" I called out as I approached.

"Lady Katarina, it's been a while," a voice to my side responded. When I turned, I came face to face with a brown-haired, grey-eyed youth. He was a very plain-looking person, and it took me a moment to recognize him — but he, too, was someone I knew very well.

"Raphael! You're participating in the festival too?"

"Yes. I am in charge of curating the items presented for sale at the festival, you see," Raphael Wolt replied, with his gentle, fleeting smile.

Up until the previous year, he had been a student at the academy, and was even the Student Council President. But due to everything that had happened last year, Raphael had to leave the academy, and

41

was now working at the Magical Ministry's research facility on the campus.

After that incident, he had discarded his false name and started a new life. Because he originally stood out so much with his charming personality and head full of red hair, he had taken on the guise of an unremarkable, brown-haired young man instead.

"I see you're working hard!" Given that the incident wasn't exactly caused by his own will, Raphael had decided to work for the Ministry, and it seemed that he was doing well for himself.

"Yes. I am at the bottom of the food chain, after all, and there is much work to be done." Although the work that Raphael described seemed incredibly complicated, he also sounded surprisingly energetic. Ever since he had gone back to being his old self, he seemed a lot brighter and more cheerful than before.

As we stood discussing Raphael's current situation, Maria soon spotted us and made her way to where we stood. "I am very glad that you are here to visit, Lady Katarina. Here... this is your share," she said, offering to me some of her homemade snacks. At my request, Maria had used the crops I had grown to make snacks to sell at the festival.

"Wow! Thanks for setting some aside for me! How were the sales?"

"Of course, Lady Katarina. Honestly... I was worried, thinking that the snacks I made would not sell at all. But thanks to you, Lady Katarina, I am almost completely sold out." Maria gestured to her product stand, and just as she said, only a few remained — only two to three small packages. Although there was still plenty of time left in the festival, her goods had sold that well already.

"They must have been popular! Of course, since they're your homemade snacks, Maria."

"No, this is thanks to your assistance as well, Lady Katarina. After all, you spread the word far and wide, didn't you?"

True, I had made it a point to tell everyone I knew. After all, this entire idea was mine to begin with. I'd wanted to put my back into it and help make the treats too, but...

A few times while I was helping bake, the snacks had caught fire. The fire even spread to other parts of the kitchen. And another time, a small explosion erupted in the pot I was using for some strange reason, and it made a huge mess.

Regardless of my mistakes, however, Maria would smile at me angelically, saying, "Ah, it's your first time, Lady Katarina. It's quite alright."

The staff in charge of the kitchen, however, didn't seem to share Maria's optimism. "Please, retrieve Katarina Claes this very instant!" they pleaded — and their words eventually reached the ears of my brother. Keith soon arrived, and, dragging me by the back of my collar, cleanly hauled me out of the kitchen and into my quarters.

But... even so... there has to be something I can do! I'd thought. I offered to help with the wrapping, but I wasn't very craft-oriented, and soon made a mess of the wrapping paper. Even so, Maria merely said the same thing, again with her same angelic smile, "Ah, it's your first time, Lady Katarina. It's quite alright." Soon, the amount of damaged wrapping paper was arranged into two large stacks.

It was then that Jeord intervened, retrieving and confiscating the rest of the papers from my hands. "Katarina. It is a waste of paper, as you can see. You have done enough, no?"

In the end, I was hardly able to help with anything. Maria, the sweet girl she was, decided to task me with the role of food tester instead. Though... all I had to do for that was eat the snacks that she made.

43

Ugh... I'm sorry I'm so useless, I'd thought. *But... Maria really is an angel in the flesh. I wish I could take her as my bride.* And with that, I was told to taste the finished treats — and oh, they were so, so delicious. So delicious that I simply kept on eating until I ate far too much.

Before I knew it, all the prototype snacks had been consumed by none other than yours truly... and Alan got annoyed at me. "Hey! What are we going to do with you, eating all of it like that?" he said, confiscating the other samples.

So in the end, I suggested an idea... and then couldn't help with any part of it. I continued to think and think about what I could do to help, but I drew a blank.

I asked Keith about it, and he promptly said, "Well then, how about you simply raise public awareness of our little venture?"

It was a great idea. I made my way around campus, desperately extolling the virtues of Maria's baking. Even so, the sale of Maria's snacks couldn't possibly be because of my advertising alone.

"Well, I did advertise. But the snacks wouldn't have sold like this if they weren't so delicious! The reason they're so popular is because they taste good!"

"...Thank you very much, Lady Katarina..." Maria said, a slight blush tinting her cheeks as she smiled faintly at me. She was so lovely that I felt like one look from her would be enough to charm the heart of any man in the world.

Ahh... Maria is so, so cute! If I were a man, I would ask for her hand in marriage in a heartbeat! As I continued to daydream, however...

"Come to think of it, Lady Campbell has decided to sign up at the Ministry, or so I hear..." Raphael said casually. This was something I had never heard of before.

"Wha?! Maria… you're going to work for the Ministry?"

"Ah, yes. I have decided to join the Ministry after graduation."

"Is… Is that so? But Maria… didn't you say during your first year that you wanted to return home after graduation and live a quiet life?"

Maria was, from what I understood, one of the few Wielders of Light in the kingdom. What I didn't know was the fact that her magic was significantly powerful even amongst this small number, and that she had received an invitation from the Ministry to join their ranks after graduation.

Didn't she say during her first year that she wanted to go home and live a quiet life? Did something happen to change her mind?

"Well… It is true, that was what I had thought shortly after enrolling in the academy, that I would simply return home and live a quiet life… but…" Then, a familiar look suddenly entered Maria's eyes — it was a look of strong, unwavering resolve. "If I did that, then I could no longer be by your side."

"Hm?" I could only stare blankly, not understanding her words. Maria, however, simply smiled gently.

"Just like I asked during the graduation ceremony last year, Lady Katarina, I would like to stay by your side. However… even if I am a Wielder of Light, I am but a commoner. I need a certain degree of social standing to stand by you — given that you are a noble, and the daughter of Duke Claes. And so I decided that I would join the Ministry, and attain the position I require."

Maria's words were almost like a proposal. For some reason I felt incredibly embarrassed. "…A-Ah… Right. Thank you, Maria. I… um. I am very happy." *Wow… I really am blushing.* I could feel the heat radiating from my face.

Perhaps due to my reaction, Maria's face was soon bright red as well. Turning to face each other, we smiled, each blushing and equally embarrassed. It was almost like Maria and I were a couple!

"Ah... do excuse me. I hate to interrupt the private world that the two of you have conjured... but I am present as well... yes?"

"Ah... oh, Raphael. A private world...?" Raphael's exasperated gaze soon dragged me back to reality. *That was dangerous, terribly dangerous indeed! Maria is simply too lovable... I was about to fall through the gates of a forbidden world!*

In fact, I was just one step away from saying *"Maria. Please... be my bride."* As expected of an otome game's true protagonist, Maria's charm was nothing to scoff at.

"To think that the motivation for you joining the Ministry, the apple of this kingdom's eye... is to be with Lady Katarina. As expected of you, Lady Campbell."

"I do understand that my reasons for joining the Ministry may be... improper. But even so, I intend to give it my all once I join its ranks. I will be in your care," Maria said, her tone serious and determined as she addressed her future senior at the Ministry, Raphael.

"I do not think that wanting to be close to someone important to you constitutes impropriety. After all, I would have done the same thing had I been in your position. However..."

"However?"

"Even if you do join the Ministry, Lady Katarina will marry Prince Jeord upon graduation. She will then become very busy, and it is unlikely that we will be able to see her often, as we do now."

"Wha?!" Maria and I both had the same look on our faces — the shock of a sudden realization. Raphael seemed equally surprised at the sight of this, as if he was saying *"Lady Campbell is one thing, but you're shocked by this too, Lady Katarina?!"*

"That… That's right… Lady Katarina is Prince Jeord's fiancée… She will immediately become his bride after graduation, and spend her days in the castle. We may not be able to see her then. I don't think I would like that very much…"

"Yes… if this goes on, I have to marry Jeord and become a royal. That would be bad… I'm barely making it as the daughter of a duke, but a royal…!"

Raphael continued looking at the two of us, somewhat troubled by our onset of depression upon realizing where we stood. "…Have you considered joining the Ministry as well, Lady Katarina?"

"Huh? I can do that? Actually, does joining the Ministry mean I wouldn't have to get married anymore?" Raphael's statement had me completely hooked. Slowly, he began feeding me the details.

"Basically, it is possible for one to join the ranks of the Ministry with the recommendation of a staff member with considerable social standing. While I do not think that simply joining the Ministry would cancel the entire engagement, the Ministry is only second to the king himself when it comes to political power. I hardly think that you would be dragged off to the castle immediately."

I see! So if I join the Ministry, I can further delay the marriage! And if I delay it long enough, Jeord will certainly fall for Maria or some other splendid noble lady… With that, I would be freed from my role! Alright, Katarina Claes! Let's aim to sign on with the Magical Ministry!

…Or at least, that's what I wanted to do, but… I was so, so bad at magic. In fact, the only spell that I could use was Earth Raiser.

"Um… Raphael. As you may know, my magical capability is… depressingly low…"

"Ah, about that. While it is indeed true that there are many in the Ministry who have high magical capability, there are equally many who are not as magically gifted. After all, we do not exactly turn away those who are simply interested in magic."

"Is that so?! That's great! Well then, I'll do my best. But didn't you say that I needed a letter of recommendation from an important person in the Ministry?"

Honestly, the only one I knew within the Ministry was Raphael. I could possibly speak with Father and have him use his connections to get me a letter of recommendation… but would such a thing even be accepted by the Ministry in the first place?

"Ugh… Then this will be really difficult, won't it? After all, no one would give someone like me a recommendation…" *It was such a great suggestion too!* I sighed, resigning myself to my fate once more.

Raphael, however, smiled somewhat suggestively. "Don't be so sad, Lady Katarina. There is in fact… someone who would write a letter of recommendation for you."

"…Really?!"

"In truth, my superior has become most interested in you, and would surely write a letter for you in a heartbeat."

"Your… superior? And this person, they know of me?"

"Yes. I do believe that she is likely to greet you sooner or later. After all, she did mention wanting to speak with you, Lady Katarina."

"Hmm… well, what kind of person is she?"

"I would describe her as having quite the individualistic streak. But I see her as a very kind person as well."

"Um, excuse me!" Maria said, forcefully interrupting the conversation Raphael and I were having. Maria wasn't normally the kind of person to do things like this, but she seemed kind of desperate.

"Wh-What is it, Maria? What happened? You look so…"

"U-Um. Well… if we were to summarize what we've just learned… if Raphael's superior would indeed write you a letter of recommendation, and you enter the Magical Ministry… then… then! Then we would be together forever!"

"That would be so, yes," Raphael said. His gentle smile seemed to wash away Maria's agitation, and soon she was smiling happily.

"Lady Katarina, let's join the ranks of the Ministry together. I will do what I can to help! Please, you must, oh you must!" Maria clasped my hands in hers — her eyes were sparkling.

Raphael, too, raised his hand, encouraging us from the sidelines. "I will help too, of course."

"Oh?! Th-Thank you so much!"

"Well let's do this then, we'll work hard together!" Maria said, her passion burning fiercely.

With our discussion done, I left Maria and Raphael behind, heading to the classmates that I had split off from a while ago. *Come to think of it… I should have asked more about Raphael's boss. Hmm. Well, I suppose I can just ask next time.*

With that, I finally met up with my friends, who had apparently bought a large number of items from the sale area.

"I purchased an embroidered handkerchief."

"Earrings and a necklace for me."

"I bought a plush toy."

Each of the girls held something cute in their hands to take home as happy memories of the school festival. They seemed to be having fun.

As for me… I looked down at the bags hanging from my arms. There was only… food. It would be gone as soon as I ate it, and wouldn't make for much of a souvenir. "…I suppose I should purchase something as a memory, too."

My classmates and friends all smiled.

"Oh, yes, how wonderful!"

"You should, Lady Katarina."

Now then... I wanted to buy something, but now that I was actually here, I wasn't quite sure what I wanted. Honestly, I couldn't envision myself liking any of the embroidered items, an accessory, or some plush toy. With the exception of things that were featured in the romance novels I read, of course.

As I stood, thinking, one of my friends pointed something out to me. "How about that piece, Lady Katarina?"

"Hmm...? A brooch?" So it was. While the brooch itself wasn't anything out of the ordinary, the blue stone embedded in its center was truly beautiful. I picked it up, and almost instantly, its color changed.

"Wow! The stone became... azure!" Seeing my surprise, the merchant kindly explained that this particular stone changed colors when brought up to the light.

"I picked it up earlier too. It's so pretty! And I was so surprised when it changed colors in my hands. And then I thought... the color of the stone in the light is most reminiscent of the color of your eyes, Lady Katarina." For some reason, the friend who had recommended the brooch to me blushed slightly as she said this. My other friends and classmates all seemed to agree.

"It's true! How wonderful, that it is the same color as your eyes!"

"It's beautiful. It really suits you."

"I-Is that so...?" While I myself had never thought much about my azure eyes, it was nice to hear that others thought they were beautiful.

In the end, I purchased the brooch with the blue stone thanks to the recommendations of my friends. The merchant handed me the brooch, now neatly packed in a small bag. I placed it in my pocket, and our group soon moved on to yet another venue.

Our next destination was the academy's magical showcase area, where students who wielded Wind, Fire, Water, and Earth Magic showed off their abilities to an audience. After all, advancing the development of magic was one of the academy's main aims.

Stationed at this important area were Prince Jeord and his twin brother, Prince Alan. The two of them should be waiting nearby. By now the events of the festival had moved into their final stages, so we quickened our pace, hoping to reach our destination a little faster.

Upon our arrival, I found myself gasping in praise. "Wow... that's something."

A jet of water was sprouting up from a pond, much like a fountain, creating a rainbow in the sky. Carvings and statues made of earth changed their forms in the blink of an eye, and dancing, vibrant flames waltzed through the air. Small hurricanes picked up flower petals, scattering them to the winds. It was a scene right out of a fairy tale — a wonderful and magical sight. I was once again struck by the fact that this place was indeed a kingdom of magic.

Although I'd been planning to find Jeord quickly and give him the gifts I'd brought, I found myself entranced by the mystical sight before me. It was too wonderful to look away — all I could do was stand there, staring at the displays in a trance. It was just too beautiful.

"I see you have come at last, Katarina." As I remained lost in my thoughts, I heard a voice call out from beside me. I turned to find a familiar blue-eyed, blonde-haired prince. Jeord stood next to me, smiling as always.

"Ah, Prince Jeord. I'm sorry for taking so long..." Since I'd stopped at so many places and done so many things at the festival, I'd arrived here considerably late. *Well... I suppose the main reason is the amount of time I spent at the food stands in the first place...*

"I forgive you, Katarina, seeing as you actually made it here before the end of the festival. Knowing you... you most likely got too excited at the food stands, and ended up spending a disproportionate amount of time there, no?"

"Ah?!" *No way! I had expected Keith to find out, more or less, but Jeord can see through me that well too... I suppose we have spent the last nine or so years together.*

"I am so sorry... I was distracted by the delicious food..." Since Jeord had already deduced the truth, I had no choice but to fess up and apologize. It would be terrifying if I somehow managed to upset this particularly sadistic prince.

"It is quite alright, as you have spent your time with these female classmates of yours. However... I would not forgive similar excursions with other men..."

Hmm? Jeord had mumbled something towards the end, but I couldn't quite catch it. For some reason, the atmosphere became somewhat tense. I could feel goosebumps running down my back.

The classmates who had accompanied me up until this point turned to leave, not wanting to interrupt our conversation. "It would be most unbecoming of us to intrude, Lady Katarina. We shall make our way around the venue for now."

Wait, everyone! Don't leave me with this black-hearted sadist prince... who's currently radiating some strange aura! Oh, my friends! Come back to me! I thought, watching the fading silhouettes of my friends with a heavy heart. However, I could see someone approaching from another direction — my savior, surely, who would do something about this strange and tense atmosphere.

"Oh, it's you two. So you're finally here? Thought you wouldn't make it, see. After you said all that about 'I'll come by with gifts!' this morning too... thought you wouldn't get here, being so late and all." With his silver hair and blue eyes, the wild and haughty Prince Alan had arrived on the scene.

"I apologize... A bunch of things slowed me down along the way." While Jeord had seen through me almost instantly, I thought something vague might pull the wool over Alan's eyes. He was, after all, quite dense when it came to these things.

"That right? I figured you ended up eating endlessly at the stands and forgot all about the time."

"..." Even the blockheaded Prince Alan knew exactly what had happened. For some reason, I felt a wave of gloom spread through me. I decided to change the subject by presenting the food I'd brought.

"Here, for you. Please try them," I said as I took out some bread I'd bought from the stands and a packet of Maria's homemade snacks. Maria had just given them to me, but I decided to offer them up as an apology for being so late.

"Ah, these are the baked goods Maria made, yes? How was it, did they sell?" Jeord inquired, immediately noticing the familiar packaging.

"Yes, they were very popular. In fact, they'd almost sold out by the time I got there."

"Is that so? That is good to hear, Katarina," Jeord replied, smiling faintly.

That smile... I could feel my womanly intuition calling out to me once more. Before I'd realized it, Jeord had been oh-so-casually calling Maria by her first name. He was worried about if Maria's snacks sold or not... And the look of relief on his face when I told him they nearly sold out... This was unmistakably...

This is it! Jeord has completely fallen for Maria! Although Fortune Lover's *scenario has already ended, he was fated to fall in love with Maria from the very beginning! Right, that's obvious! After all, Maria is simply overflowing with charm, enough to even make my heart skip... even though I'm a girl too.*

"Maria's snack stand... you were quite enthusiastic in your support for her, no? Katarina...? Are you listening to me?"

Right... now that this is clear to me, I have even more reason to quickly enter the Magical Ministry, delay my engagement, and cheer for Jeord and his quest for Maria's love.

"...Again, Katarina...?"

"Hey, Katarina Claes! Lady Dimwit! No good... she isn't listening at all."

Ah, but... what about Maria? We hadn't had any conversations about love, or who she liked, since that graduation ceremony. I still didn't know if there was anyone she had fallen for. There was, perhaps, the possibility that she had started liking another potential love interest who wasn't Jeord. *Hmm... I should look further into this next time— Ouch!*

"Wh-What are you doing?!" I glared at the one who had suddenly rapped me on the head. It was painful, and I was shocked by the suddenness.

The culprit, Alan, simply dismissed my protests. "Your fault for not listening when people are talking to you."

Ugh... I guess he's right. I'd gotten distracted by thoughts of Jeord and Maria and had become lost in my own world.

"Th-Then all you had to do was say something! You didn't have to rap me on the head!"

"What are you blathering about, dummy? I did that already! It's your fault for not reacting at all." With that, Alan placed a hand on my head again and messed up my hair.

Ungh, this barbarian! I went through all that effort to have my hair done for me, and now he messed it all up! Just as I was about to retaliate with a well-placed counterattack...

"That is quite enough, Alan. I would strongly prefer that you do not touch her so casually." Before I could even raise a hand in retaliation, Jeord had firmly grasped Alan's arm, coming between us as he did so.

Jeord had intervened to break up the little scuffle between Alan and I... or so it seemed. However, it felt like the atmosphere was becoming even stranger and tenser... was it just my imagination?

"...Ahh, Jeord... you're always like this," Alan sighed, his arm still in his brother's grasp. "Aren't you being a little too uptight? Keep that up and you're going to be disliked eventually... That's what Mary says."

"Do inform Lady Mary that her concern is most misplaced."

The two princes now stood, facing each other... for some reason, the atmosphere grew even heavier than it was just now. *Huh? Did my scuffle with Alan set off an argument between them? What should I do?* I could only stand there, feeling anxious about these strange developments.

"Jeord, Alan." Someone had called out to the two princes standing before me. Turning my head to the origin of the voice, I saw two couples walk towards us. The person leading them was smiling and waving, so it seemed that he was the one who had called out to them just now.

He had so casually called Jeord and Alan by their first names, with no titles… I wondered who this person was. He seemed similar to someone I knew. This suspicion was confirmed by what Jeord said next: "Elder Brother Jeffrey, I see you have come to visit."

Oh, I see! Jeord's older brother! Now that I looked at him again, his silver hair and blue eyes did remind me of Alan.

Jeord greeted the young man following after Jeffrey as well. "And you too, Elder Brother Ian."

Huh?! The one behind is his older brother too? With his blonde hair and blue eyes, he did have a striking resemblance to Jeord.

Right… the four princes of the kingdom were these four brothers. Jeffrey, the one who looked very much like Alan, was the first prince. Ian, who looked like Jeord, was the second. It seemed like someone had told me all this before…

"Oh, if it isn't Lady Katarina Claes. Long time no see."

I froze up at the prince's greeting. *Huh? Been a while? Have I even met this person before?*

Noticing my sudden rigidity, Jeord leaned in ever so slightly, whispering, "Come now Katarina, we all met at my birthday party once."

Ah, that's right! Come to think of it… Jeord did introduce me to them then. I had seen their faces, but then ended up forgetting all about it.

"Ah, yes. It has... been quite a while indeed, Prince Jeffrey, Prince Ian..." After returning his greeting, I turned to the two women who had accompanied the princes here. One of them had long, black hair and blue eyes. She had all the right curves in the right places, and seductive charm oozed from her being. She was exceedingly beautiful too, with an attractive face to match her body.

The other woman was the exact opposite of the black-haired beauty. Instead, she had an air of refined simplicity about her. Her hair and eyes were a gentle brown, and while she wasn't ravishing or stunning, her small frame and large eyes made her seem like a small animal. Something about her appearance made one want to protect her.

Judging by how the two of them were being escorted by the princes, I assumed that they were most likely their fiancées, but I didn't know their names. As Jeord had said just now, I did meet with all of them at least once... but only once. I couldn't possibly remember their faces or names. I desperately tried to recall my memories from two years ago, but it would seem that they had already left on a long, long journey... *What should I do?*

Jeord, sensing my peril, subtly whispered words of advice to my ear once more. "The one that Jeffrey is escorting, with the black hair, is Lady Susanna Randall. The one that Ian is escorting, with the brown hair, is Lady Selena Berg. They are both the fiancées of my brothers."

Thank you, Prince Jeord! Reliable as always.

"It's good to see you Lady Randall, Lady Berg," I said, giving the two as ladylike of a greeting as I possibly could.

"Been a while, yes. Lady Katarina, please just call me Susanna," the black-haired, seductive beauty said, her red lipstick curling up into a friendly smile.

"It is good to see you. Please... do call me Selena." The refined, yet cute girl with the small frame followed suit, bowing her head slightly as she greeted me in return. While they were both fiancées to princes, the contrast between them couldn't be any more stark.

"What brings you to this place today, brothers?" asked Jeord.

Jeffrey answered with a jovial tone, almost beaming as he did so. "Why, to witness my beloved little brothers' amazing exhibition, of course!" His words were unnecessarily theatrical.

Jeord stared at him coldly before turning to his other brother. "So... how about we come clean, Ian?"

"Of course. We are here on royal business. A routine examination... inspection of the Academy of Magic. I suppose Jeffrey is here on similar grounds as well."

"You suppose? Ah. I see that you two have not arrived together."

"It goes without saying. We had just crossed paths with each other, coincidentally, moments ago," Prince Ian replied, with calmness that was almost jarring when compared with Jeffrey's theatrical statement.

I had thought that the two royal fiancées were different... but it would seem like the princes had contrasting personalities as well. Jeffrey, who very much resembled Alan, always had a smile on his face, and seemed like he was always ready to flirt with anyone. Ian, who resembled Jeord, was the opposite — always stoic, with a serious look about him.

So... a flirt, a stoic, a black-hearted sadist prince, and a haughty, dense prince... the royal household had quite the variety of personalities. Even so, they were both princes, right? Why weren't they together? Did they not get along? I made a mental note to ask Jeord about this later.

Unlike Ian, who was now calmly explaining his assignment to Jeord in a deadpan tone, Jeffrey had decided to annoy his youngest brother instead. "Huh? You're both no fun, Jeord, Ian! Well then... come here, Alan! Big Brother is here to see you!"

"H-Hey! Stop it. Don't hug me," Alan said, with an expression of sincere distaste on his face as Jeffrey clung onto him.

I couldn't help but feel a little sorry for Jeffrey, who didn't seem well-liked by his brothers at all. But Susanna, who was standing opposite me all this time, started laughing softly to herself. "Oh, how silly, Prince Jeffrey. You seem to be having fun. Well then, Lady Katarina... would you like a hug like that from me, too?" she said, out of nowhere.

"Wha?!" *Wh-What is this glamorous woman talking about, all of a sudden?* In fact, her hips were swaying from side to side as she approached me! She was getting closer! *I-Is this woman serious?* "Ah, um. Uh..." Panicking, I could hardly form words.

Susanna, however, simply looked at me with amusement, her eyes narrowing like a cat as she smiled. "Mhmhm. Alas, I was only joking, Lady Katarina. I would not take you into my arms without warning."

"Ah... right. Right." I was shocked... I had taken her little joke seriously. Alas, I could not understand the jokes of impossibly glamorous women.

Lowering her voice to a whisper, Susanna continued. "...Not yet, anyway. Not now," she said, her smile growing broader.

I started panicking again. *Huh? That was another joke, right?*

Just then, the sound of bells rang out through the air. *Clang! Clang!* It would seem that there wasn't much time left in the festival.

Once the event was over, the schedule would move on to the ball that was scheduled for that night.

"Ah. Do excuse us. We have to head to the stage soon," Jeord said as the bells continued tolling. The play by the student council was the last event before the dance ball. This was why Jeord was heading off — he and the other members should be gathering near the stage now, ready to show off their acting skills.

"Ohh? A performance, Jeord? I would like to see it too, oh yes."

"Enough with the tomfoolery, Jeffrey. We're heading back."

"Whaaa…? You really are no fun, Ian. Actually, Ian… you're heading back with me?"

"As I said, enough nonsense. There is no way I could return with you."

Jeffrey was currently being scolded by Ian, and I couldn't tell which one was the older of the two princes anymore. However… the fact that they could speak like this suggested that they got along well. But still, they wouldn't return to the castle together? So they didn't get along after all? I couldn't wrap my head around it.

"Well then, Lady Katarina. See you later," the bewitching beauty said, with the slightest hint of a smile.

The cute, meek girl on the other hand lowered her head again, muttering a curt goodbye. "Farewell."

"See ya!"

"Well then. Do excuse us."

And with that, the two princes and their fiancées were gone. It was perhaps worth noting that the two older princes did bring a bunch of gifts with them and had left them with Jeord. Despite all they'd said, I supposed they did intend to visit him. While I wanted to ask Jeord more about the princes and their relationship in general, it was already time for the play, and I, too, rushed off to the stage area.

By the time I reached the stage, all members of the council except Jeord and Alan were already gathered. Some of the female students already had their costumes on.

Alright! I'll change too, into these light and casual clothes I prepared beforehand to assist my friends backstage. That was when it happened — when I had my clothes bundled in my hands, ready to head off and change.

"It's terrible! One of the actresses is unwell, and can no longer perform!" one of the students assisting backstage said. Apparently one of the girls who was due to play a part in the play had suddenly felt unwell, collapsed, and had to be carried off to the infirmary. Thankfully, the diagnosis was nothing to be alarmed at, she was simply a little tired, and would recover with some rest. However... the play was about to begin, and she was unable to participate.

"We have no choice. We will simply have to find a replacement," Jeord said, upon receiving the news from the assistant. He then turned to the gathered members of the council. With that announcement, however, all the other students assisting in the production of the play averted their eyes.

But of course they would. After all, the student council was wildly popular in the academy. All the members of the council were highly attractive, and most of them had a fair number of fans. To have someone who looked relatively normal stand amongst these dazzling people... While it was not exactly impossible, it was very hard to do. Following the crowd, I averted my eyes too, but...

"Well then... in that case, wouldn't Lady Katarina be fit for the role?" one of the other students said. She was also assisting backstage. Although she didn't announce her statement loudly, the area we were gathered in was now deathly quiet — and everyone heard her. And then...

"I, too, think that Lady Katarina would be fit for the role."

"I feel that only Lady Katarina can stand with the rest of the student council members…"

"Yes, if it's Lady Katarina, the audience and other students would be most satisfied as well."

Voice after voice amongst my fellow backstage assistants rose up, almost all at once. *W-Wait. I can't do it! It's impossible! After all, I've only played rocks… or trees… it's impossible for me to play an actual person! To begin with… how could someone like me, with my villainess face, stand amongst the glamorous members of the council?*

"I… I c-can't…" I said, objecting to this sudden role thrust upon me.

The other students around me, however, refused to hear it. "I think it would be best for Lady Katarina to play this role," they said.

U-Ugh… Someone, please! Stand with me and tell these people that I simply can't do it! Now that it had come to this… Jeord! Jeord would surely say *"It is all but impossible for Katarina."* I turned to Jeord expectantly, only for him to smile at me.

"Well then, Katarina. I leave it in your capable hands," he said, placing a hand on my shoulder — and that was the final say in the matter.

And so it came to be that I ended up unexpectedly performing in the student council's play…

It's impossible! There's no way I can do it! I thought as I continued to fidget. Around me, however, the preparations were well under way. Before I knew it, I had been fit snugly into my costume and handed my lines. Fortunately… or perhaps unfortunately, the student who had passed out had about the same physique as I did, and I fit into her costume with no issues. I could no longer escape.

Although I had seen the council practice countless times, I simply had no ability when it came to memorizing lines. As such, I buried myself in my lines furiously.

"Do not worry, Katarina. You don't have many lines to begin with," Jeord said, almost casually. I would prefer if Jeord didn't put me in the same boat as him, though. After all, I wasn't a high-spec all-rounder like he was. Even if I did somehow memorize these lines, I would simply forget all of them when I stood on stage — the gazes of the audience would make me too nervous.

Ugh... now that's come to this, I have to rely on a cheat sheet! Yes, we shall do that, Katarina Claes! I started desperately copying my lines down on a tiny piece of paper. With this, my cunning preparations were complete — and the play began.

"I am very happy to be able to stand on the same stage as you, Lady Katarina," Maria said, smiling as she walked out onto the stage. She was, of course, playing the role of the protagonist. I could only silently see her off as I furiously wrote lines in the palm of my hand.

The content of the play was much like the story of "Cinderella" that I was familiar with in my previous life. A play was modeled off a folk tale of sorts, basically, chosen so that the younger siblings of the academy's students who were in the audience would be able to understand and enjoy the story.

As such, even I, who usually distanced myself from difficult or complicated stories, knew the play's general outline. In fact, its plot was pretty much identical to Cinderella's. It was a story about a noble girl who was mistreated by her stepmother and older stepsister, and treated like a servant. Even so, she was a positive and gentle girl, who got along very well with the servants of her family, as well as the townsfolk.

One day, a ball was held at a nearby castle. The girl's stepmother and stepsister were busy with their preparations, fitting themselves into luxurious outfits. The noble girl could only look on, sad and envious of her stepmother and sister. The servants and townsfolk, being aware of this, prepared a dress for her as well, keeping it a secret from her mother and sister.

On the day of the ball, the servants dressed up the noble girl after her mother and sister had left, allowing her to go to the ball as well. When she arrived, a young man called out to her, inviting her to dance. The girl's heart was captivated by the gentle and handsome youth. They danced until the ball was nearing its end — but it was then that the girl caught sight of her mother and sister. Panicking, she escaped from the ballroom, and in her haste left a single shoe behind.

The youth, a prince from a certain kingdom, had danced with the girl and fallen head over heels for her. He picked up her forgotten shoe and began searching for the girl that he had danced with. Word soon spread throughout the land: "She who is able to put on this shoe shall become the prince's bride." It was a shoe that only that girl could put on — and she would eventually marry the handsome prince... so went the story.

Well, other than the fact that there was no magic involved, and that the shoe in question wasn't made of glass, it was more or less an identical story to Cinderella. Jeord was the prince, of course, and the protagonist was Maria. For some reason, Mary was playing the stepmother. My role was that of the mean stepsister, who would often bully and mistreat Maria's character.

This really was a fitting role for Katarina, who looked every bit the part of an evil noble lady. *No... impossible. Could it be? Although the events of* Fortune Lover *ended safely... I'm now forced into bullying Maria?* I was filled with a sense of unease.

The stepsister character mainly appeared in the first half of the play to bully Maria. Once that was over, she would show up in a short scene at the dance ball, and finally when the shoe was fitted onto the protagonist's foot. She didn't have many scenes. All I had to do was somehow get through the first half…

Shortly after Maria went out on the stage, it was my turn. The stepmother character that Mary played was calling for me. With a final series of letters scrawled on my palm, I swallowed deeply, heading out onto the stage.

And now… I was in the spotlight. On stage. I could see a seemingly endless ocean of audience members before me — they filled my field of vision. At this particular point in time, the worst scenario that I had envisioned came true… the lines that I had struggled so desperately to remember all disappeared from my mind.

I hadn't made much headway memorizing them to begin with, so I suppose there was no helping it. But I had anticipated that this would happen — and that was why I'd prepared this little sheet of paper. *How fortunate that I prepared a cheat sheet, indeed!* Slowly, I began to withdraw the small piece of paper hidden in the folds of my dress… or at least, I tried.

Huh? Where… where is it? I can't find it… I searched desperately in the fold where I had hidden the cheat sheet, but to no avail. *Wh-What should I do?* I was overcome by a wave of despair. I looked downwards. Perhaps I had dropped it? But there was nothing at my feet. I turned ever so slightly… and there, by the curtains, was the small piece of paper that I had dropped.

U-Ugh! My cheat sheet! I dropped it by the curtains… what a terrible mistake! Now that I was on stage, it was impossible for me to turn back. I was in a bind. A most dire, life-threatening bind. In addition, due to my fidgeting, a strange silence had fallen upon the stage.

There was no other choice. I simply had to do it. However, I couldn't remember my lines. Still… this scene was where my character bullied Maria's protagonist character. That was all I had to do, right? Well then… I would have to become the villainess, Katarina Claes, here and now. There was no other way.

Up until last year, I had been desperately taking notes about *Fortune Lover*, and memorizing whatever I could at every opportunity. As such, I could easily recall how Katarina had bullied the protagonist. *Alright! Let's do this. This stage now belongs to the villainess, Katarina Claes.*

And so I used lines from *Fortune Lover*, mercilessly lashing out at Maria's protagonist character. Things like "Honestly. Do you really not know your place?" and "Someone like you should just lie down in the dirt and stay there. After all, that suits you best."

Maria and Mary were both momentarily stunned at my lines — after all, they weren't anything like what was in the script. However, the two of them, being as capable as they were, quickly grasped the situation and improvised. After this scene, I made sure to subtly hide the cheat sheet in my hands.

With that, the curtains finally fell on the first play that I had ever participated in.

"Lady Katarina… your lines, your acting when you bullied the protagonist… most wonderful."

"Really! She had this terrifying aura about her."

"To think that Lady Katarina is capable of such acting… it was almost as if she were someone else! How unexpected…"

"You must have quite the talent for acting, Lady Katarina! Truly splendid!"

For reasons unknown to me, my little performance won great praise from my classmates and friends. In fact, even acquaintances of mine praised my effort. Apparently, the first few lines that I had delivered were seen as intentional ad-libbing. Me using Katarina's lines from *Fortune Lover* and role-playing as her was apparently very well received. Even Maria and Mary, who were thrown off by my strange ad-libbing, had nothing but praise for my performance.

At first, I was humbled by all the praise. All I did was copy what Katarina did in *Fortune Lover*... It really wasn't anything special. But now that everyone was congratulating me, I slowly felt myself riding high on that wave of praise. I often got ahead of myself in this way... and my head was already in the clouds.

I should be aiming to be an actress in the future, then! Not just someone in the Magical Ministry. Upon returning to the waiting room, I started posing in front of the mirror — poses which the stepsister character had been taking on stage.

Still elated at my acting achievements, I struck a particularly impressive pose before the mirror, before stuffing my face full of the snacks that Jeord's brothers had offered us.

It was then that one of the backstage assistant students called out to me. "Lady Katarina, you should be leaving for the ball soon. The other members of the council are calling for you," she said.

I had simply intended to do a series of poses and eat some snacks, but I ended up taking longer than I'd expected. Quite some time had passed. The ball was the very last event of the school festival. Jeord would be escorting me, and I had promised my brother and friends that I would dance with them too. They wouldn't be happy if I was late.

The academy was dark at this point. The backstage assistant student who so kindly informed me of the time, however, offered to guide me. "I shall guide you to the venue, Lady Katarina," she said, holding a lantern and leading me along. Under normal circumstances I would have returned to my quarters by this time, so I wasn't used to seeing the academy in the dark.

It was fitting for a school festival at an academy filled with nobles to end with a ball. I supposed the equivalent in my previous life would be a school campfire and folk dance. *Ahh... in the end, I couldn't have my favorite yakisoba or okonomiyaki.* I was able to eat all kinds of delicious food in exchange, but now that I got it in my head, I couldn't give up now. *I should ask the chefs to prepare some for me next time I'm back home.*

As I continued to dream about what delicious food I could eat, the student leading me towards the ball suddenly stopped. *Huh? This is where the ball is being held? There's no lights anywhere...* When I stopped to look, I saw that we had ended up somewhere away from the academy. No matter how I looked at it, this couldn't possibly be where the ball was being held... Did she get lost due to how dark it was?

"Um... excuse me..." I called out to the student leading me. And then—

Suddenly, an unseen individual grasped me by the arm, and placed what seemed to be a cloth over my face. For some reason, the cloth smelled sweet. Shortly after I inhaled this strange sweetness, my entire body felt heavy, and soon, my consciousness faded away.

Before I fully passed out, I thought I heard Keith's voice softly resonating in my mind. *"I always tell you to be careful, Big Sister..."*

As a member of the student council, I, Keith Claes, was assigned to a display venue showcasing the history and magical research of our kingdom for the duration of the school festival. I smiled at a seemingly endless stream of students and their guardians. Although Big Sister said she'd come by soon, I still couldn't see her. And so I waited.

"I'll go have a look at the stands and then come back with gifts!" she'd said before heading off. It had already been a few hours since then. Even Mary Hunt, a friend of mine and fellow student council member who'd been assigned to this space, looked worried.

Well, if I had to guess, Katarina probably got distracted by all the food at the stands, started eating, and lost track of time altogether… As a result, it wasn't until later in the afternoon that the person I'd been waiting for showed up.

Upon seeing us, she broke into a wide smile, quickly approaching with her two hands full of bags of various sizes. In the end, it was just as I'd predicted — Katarina had ended up buying and eating snacks endlessly, and hence was late to our meeting.

"…I'm sorry," Katarina apologized almost immediately. Mary, however, simply responded with, "Think nothing of it, Lady Katarina. I am only glad that you are safe."

However… if I spoiled her here, she'd simply keep doing the same thing over and over again. After all, this was my Big Sister we were talking about. "Really, Big Sister. Are you not being a little too careless? You do have a habit of getting into trouble. Please be aware of that… and be more careful," I said, looking at her strictly.

Katarina's expression of remorse was almost pitiful. She had always been like this — she would often get into some sort of trouble, being the natural charmer that she was, ever since our childhood. Last year, the incident she'd been involved in could have very well cost her her life.

Even so… my amazingly dense and carefree sister had all but forgotten about it. As of late, she had been especially relaxed and careless. Although I had warned her repeatedly about Prince Jeord, who sought to make her his, my advice was not heeded, entering through her right ear and predictably leaving from her left. She would go into Jeord's quarters on her own without a second thought.

Katarina was already a grown woman. However, she seemed incapable of realizing that there were some people who saw her as an object of desire. She was completely unaware of this fact. This was why I always had to be on my guard, day after day. I had to be constantly vigilant… all for the sake of protecting her.

Although she had already had her fair share of food at the stands, Katarina decided to join us for a short tea snack. While I was worried about her eating a little too much, I was pleased that we could dine at the same table together. In truth, I'd wanted to join her on her rounds through the festival, but I was bound by tasks at the council.

Why did I join the student council, of all things? On this day, and perhaps this day alone, this particular regret filled my mind.

Katarina gazed at the sandwiches laid out on the table happily, exclaiming that they looked delicious. Her sparkling eyes and expression of anticipation was adorable.

Mary agreed with Katarina's assessment, and thanked her for bringing the food. She was smiling, clearly very pleased. Perhaps this was why I had to say what I did.

"Big Sister... did you not already have quite a lot to eat? Please eat in moderation, or you'll get a stomach ache."

"...Yes, I understand." Katarina seemed a little deflated at my words. It was a saddening sight, yes, but I had to warn her before she stuffed herself silly. This was all for Katarina's sake.

After nibbling and chewing on her seemingly delicious sandwich for a while, her eyes started darting this way and that as if she were thinking of something. *Ah... this is probably—* and before I could finish my thought, I was predictably interrupted.

"Hey, Keith... could I split the sandwiches with you? I'll have half." Katarina had blurted out the very words I had expected her to say.

"...Sure. I thought you might say that, Big Sister."

"Hooray!" Katarina, after all, really loved to eat. She was particularly interested in rare or uncommon ingredients and dishes. If she laid eyes on something rare, she simply had to eat it.

It seemed that Katarina had a certain philosophy when it came to food — she was never one to leave a meal unfinished. Other nobles, me included, often left a little bit of our meal behind. This contrasted starkly with Katarina's behavior, and although I was used to her antics at this point, parts of her still seemed a little strange.

This was because the Claes family raised its children to cherish their food — they would be fed just enough, and were educated early in their lives on the importance of food. Personally, I was fond of Katarina's strange eating habits, at least when it came to finishing food. I did feel a little sad seeing Katarina stuff herself attempting to finish everything she ate, though.

This was why I said what I did to her quite some years ago: *"If you would like to try a bit of everything, Big Sister, how about you split half of it with me? I will finish the other half for you."*

Katarina was unexpectedly delighted at my suggestion, and ever since then, we would often split our meals or dishes if we could — barring meals at public locations and venues, of course. This splitting of food, in turn, was something of a family privilege. After all, I was the only one who Katarina shared her food with… and this pleased me greatly.

"Here you go, Keith! Try some." Katarina, having sought my permission to split meals, was now delivering part of a potato salad sandwich into my mouth. It was near my lips. I hadn't noticed this — and I froze at this development.

"Is something the matter, Keith?" Katarina said, gazing curiously at my rigid expression. She didn't seem to understand the situation at hand.

Don't ask me if something's the matter, Katarina! Notice already! "A-Ah… well. Big Sister… Could we perhaps not do this in public, and in full view of others?" *Perhaps if I just calmly remind her…*

"Others? But this isn't really a public venue. Didn't you just say it was fine just moments ago?"

"Well… I didn't mean it in this particular way… that…" My words were not getting through to her! Almost immediately, I felt pierced by Mary's gaze from across the table.

"Hmm? So the two of you always do this, as long as you are not in a public space…?" Mary, her gaze dripping hostility, still managed to sport a smile as she calmly delivered her lines.

"Ah, right. When I have something that I want to taste, but can't finish it all, I usually split half of it and give it to Keith."

Yes, that's right. But perhaps we could leave the explanation at that, Big Sister. It would be dangerous to go any further.

"Is that right? And so, Lady Katarina… do you mean to say that this half portion is always fed to Master Keith's lips… with your hands?" As expected, Mary homed in on the very details I did not wish to share. I shot yet another glance at Katarina, hoping that she would understand and hold her tongue. Alas… she was oblivious to my subtle communication.

"Of course. It wasn't like that at first, but Keith asked me to feed him that way whenever we split food a while ago, so now I always do."

Mercilessly exposed. I could feel the intensity of Mary's gaze increase by several distinct degrees. There was no escaping it.

Originally, I had been satisfied just living together with her. However, due to Jeord's increasingly intense interactions with Katarina over the years, even I had issues suppressing my desires.

To begin with… I lived in the same home as Katarina. More than anyone else, I was the one who was always by her side. Honestly, it would be all too simple for something to happen between us. It was possible, yes… but I did not have the courage to pursue such developments.

To make things worse, Katarina had slowly become more ladylike as the days passed, and I could no longer touch her casually like I did in the past. With her sweet, fragrant scent… her soft skin and body — recently I found my heartbeat increasing exponentially, and my body heating up when I approached her. Before I knew it, I was already avoiding her. I had been beside myself with worry all these past years.

Jeord, however, would simply lay his hands on her casually all this time. I wanted to do the same! I had never been able to embrace her the way Jeord did. And that is why I thought of this plan: If I couldn't touch her, then I could arrange so Katarina would be the one extending her hand to me! Splitting food was the perfect cover for this.

I did realize that it was pathetic at best — that I, being unable to make the appropriate advances, had to rely on the other person to do it for me. Even so, I felt a sweet sense of bliss as Katarina's hand came so close to my lips.

Katarina, however, being as dense as she was, hardly noticed my feelings for her across all these years. It goes without saying that she had never understood the true meaning behind my requests either. Even so, being fed by Katarina in such a fashion filled me with a sense of secret superiority. But to think that all this would be exposed in public, right here and now, in this way...!

"...Master Keith. Did you not agree that you would not abuse your position as a family member, and keep her all to yourself? You did, did you not?" Mary said, staring upwards at me with narrowed eyes.

While it was true that Mary and I shared a common foe in the form of Jeord, and had formed a temporary alliance... Honestly, what I asked Katarina to do was a lot more forgivable than Jeord's audacious acts! I promptly used that as an excuse.

But Mary wasn't having it. "Please do not bring Prince Jeord into this conversation, or use him as a point of reference. He is abnormal! I had thought that you were far too awkward, not even trying to hold hands... a miscalculation on my part," she said, with a cold, piercing stare that was as harsh as her words.

Lady Mary Hunt, daughter of Marquess Hunt. When I first met her nine years ago, she was a withdrawn, timid young girl without the slightest hint of self-confidence. But now she had grown into a woman with such a strong will... Well, I suppose a certain someone's influence was a significant factor.

"Lady Mary, you know I can hear you despite your muffled whispers. What a thing to say! This is the height of rudeness! Do you not also abuse the fact that you're a woman? You engage in excessive bodily contact — hugging, touching... Is that not true?"

Mary, being very fond of Katarina herself, often had her hands all over my sister — perhaps even more so than Jeord. The reason she could get away with this, of course, was that they were both women. Even so, I couldn't help but think that Lady Mary's frequency of contact was a little too extreme.

"Oh my. Abuse, Master Keith? How equally rude of you. It is most normal for girls to hug and touch each other, is it not? And then eventually... slowly... even share a bath together..."

"I must disagree, Lady Mary. What you just said cannot possibly be construed as normal."

"Alas, Master Keith. Does that not say more about you and your perspective instead?"

We were both under the same temporary banner, primarily out of our love for the same person (though I was unable to discern if Mary's love for Katarina was much like mine... or was it more of a friendly kind of love, perhaps? I didn't know). Now that our grievances were on the table, however, we simply couldn't stop arguing and snapping at each other.

To make things worse, I had been bound to all this student council work all day, and couldn't go enjoy the festival with Katarina. My dissatisfaction was at its peak. Soon enough, the argument between Mary and I rapidly worsened. And then —

"Keith... Mary. Should the time ever come to pass, I will definitely side with you both, don't you worry! Even if any mistakes are made... I will not allow this to become a romantic tragedy, like Romeo and the rest!"

Just like that, our argument was immediately dispelled by Katarina's sudden statement. *What exactly is she going on about? No... I think I know what conclusion she's arrived at. The real question is... how did she even come to such an assumption?!*

I answered Katarina's passionate, almost blazing gaze with as calm of a tone as I could muster. "Big Sister... I don't quite know what you're thinking in that head of yours — but I am very sure that whatever conclusion you've arrived at, it is most mistaken."

"I would have to agree as well, Lady Katarina. I vehemently reject such a conclusion," Mary said, equally firmly.

"...Um. Then... the love between Keith and Mary...?"

"You are most mistaken," Mary and I said at once, uncannily harmonized.

It was as I had expected — some sort of strange, inexplicable, incomprehensible misunderstanding on Katarina's part. *How, exactly, does this adoptive sister of mine come to these ludicrous conclusions? After all, she hasn't noticed any of my heartfelt feelings all this time. One day, I would very much like to look into her mind.*

More importantly, however, was a certain question I just had to ask... "Big Sister, who exactly is this 'Romeo'...?" I couldn't possibly overlook the fact that the name of some unknown mystery man had just left Katarina's lips.

I felt troubled by my own carelessness. If at all possible, I preferred that the number of rivals I had to contend with did not increase...

★★★★★★★★★

I, Nicol Ascart, had paid the Academy of Magic a visit on this day. On the surface, I was here to meet with my sister, Sophia. However, there was someone else I wanted to see even more than my sister.

Lady Katarina Claes, daughter of Duke Claes. The fiancée of my childhood friend, Jeord… and the secret object of my desires. I hardly had thoughts of snatching her from Jeord's grasp and making her mine. Now that I had graduated from the academy, however, there were few chances to see her in person. Even if it was just for a short, fleeting moment, I wanted to see her smile. I wanted to see it… badly.

Having arrived at the performance venue, I sought out my sister, and we stood near the entrance. The student performers, unhappy that I was drawing the gazes of the audience, asked us to go somewhere else. That is how I found myself in the backstage area.

In truth, Sophia and I were happy to sneak backstage. I had been aware of the stares of others ever since a young age, but even so, the intensity of these stares had become somewhat fearsome as of late. Their gazes stuck to me almost like a miasma. Even if I were to return their stares — they would almost immediately avert their eyes. It was not a good feeling.

Compared to that, Katarina would look straight at me with her aqua-blue eyes. It put me at ease, seeing myself reflected in her gaze. It filled me with bliss. I wanted to see her.

Perhaps my feelings had reached out to her somehow. Like a dazzling ray of light, Katarina appeared, illuminating the dark backstage area with her brilliant smile.

"Ah, Lady Katarina. I am glad that you have come…" Sophia said, welcoming Katarina eagerly.

My sister loved Katarina very much too. To begin with, Katarina was the reason why she was able to walk in the light with a smile.

"It is good to see you, Katarina." Just the sight of her was enough. I felt the edges of my lips curl up naturally. I was glad that I could see her, for the first time in such a long time.

"…A-Ah. Yes. You as well, Master Nicol." She was just like how she had been when I met her, with her straightforward gaze… I could feel a silent heat in my chest.

Katarina asked why we were hiding backstage, pointing out that we would draw a crowd if we were out front. Sophia answered her inquiry by dutifully explaining our debacle. She seemed somewhat down by the time she was done with her explanation. In response, Katarina reached into her bag and pulled out what appeared to be some food and gifts.

Upon receiving the gifts, Sophia's smile returned. I felt a deep sense of relief. After all, I was the reason why the smile had faded from Sophia's features in the first place. I was deeply grateful towards Katarina. Once again, she had put a smile on my sister's face.

"Come to think of it, Lady Katarina… you ended up not participating in the student council play," Sophia said suddenly.

Sophia had sent me a letter a while ago mentioning that the council was putting on a performance for the festival. I supposed she was referring to that. There was no mention of the actors and actresses featured in the performance, but I had assumed that Katarina would be participating as well. It would appear that I was mistaken.

"Ah, that. Well, I'm not really a member of the council after all, and I don't really have any acting talent."

Sophia seemed saddened by Katarina's blunt response. "Ah... I had hoped that I would see you on stage, Lady Katarina..."

"...I see. So Katarina will not be performing..." The words left my mouth before I could stop myself. I had wanted to see her stand on stage. Most regrettable.

And then, Katarina said the following: "But wouldn't it make more sense for you to star in a performance, Master Nicol? After all, you never did anything like that during your school festival. How about starring in a guest role in a short performance?"

It was as Katarina said; I had not participated in any event when the school festival was held during my time. Many of my friends were now in the council, however. My sister belonged to the council as well. If possible, I would have very much liked to assist, but...

"...Sadly, Katarina, I am incapable of acting."

"...Incapable, Master Nicol?" Katarina adopted a stunned expression at my response. Perhaps she didn't understand my words.

Before I could respond, Sophia had spoken in my stead. "Hmm... I do think so, Lady Katarina... Big Brother would be a little troubled if he had to act. Although he is an amazing person — and I would say this even if he were not my own brother — he unfortunately finds it difficult to control what emotions he shows outwardly. It is quite the flaw..."

Katarina seemed to have a better understanding of the situation upon Sophia's response. "Oh, yeah... That's right..." she said.

I felt a complex mix of emotions rise up from within me as I looked at the two. Yes, it was just how Sophia had explained. I was unable to freely express emotions on my face. To be more precise — I had tried to do so in the past, but the results were somewhat unnatural.

Back when I was still attending the academy, Katarina once made an observation: *"You don't seem to smile very much when you're around your classmates, Master Nicol."* She'd seemed curious. Although I had wanted to do so to a certain degree, it would appear that I could not smile whenever I wanted.

"Well then, Master Nicol. Please try to smile!" Katarina said, that same brilliant grin on her face.

However, it seemed fruitless. I could not do it. I came to the realization that it was simply impossible for me to smile at will; I did not have the ability to control my facial muscles in such a way. It had never been pointed out to me before, so I had not noticed it. Though, thinking back upon it, those who did meet my gaze would always quickly avert their eyes, so they probably did not get a good enough look at my face to mention it.

It was truly a pathetic tale. As such, I thought that it was simply impossible for me to act, no matter how hard I tried.

"Ah… but if it is you, Lady Katarina, a smile would surely come across Big Brother's face." Perhaps she had noticed that I was feeling down. I did not expect Sophia to say something like that. *How surprising. How could Sophia say such a thing out of the blue?*

"In that case, wouldn't it make more sense for his practice partner to be you, Sophia?" Katarina replied, evidently surprised.

"Alas… I do not have the strength. The one who can draw out Big Brother's smile is you alone, Lady Katarina."

"Ah, no, but then I wouldn't be able to either—"

"No, that is not true, Lady Katarina! Ah! How about we have Big Brother say some lines from the play right now? You can be the actress opposite him. Surely he will say these lines with a smile."

Sophia had a point. I often found myself smiling before Katarina without even noticing it. Even so... I could not possibly act just because of this. My sister, however, seemed to be in a much better mood upon hearing that her suggestion was accepted. With sparkling, eager eyes, she described to me the lines and motions of the scene in question. So I decided to humor her as well as I could. Sophia seemed to be enjoying herself... and so I listened.

It wasn't long before hesitation washed over my being. The scene that Sophia had told me to perform with Katarina was the play's climax, the scene where the characters confess their love to each other. The prince would gently run his fingers through the hair of the woman he loved. With a smile, he would hold her tight. It was one of the play's most important scenes.

In other words... I had to whisper lovingly. Into Katarina's ear. While holding her close to me. I could not do anything of the sort! It was not possible. Katarina, who was standing in a somewhat intimidating stance opposite me, however, demanded that I begin.

I did not really understand, but I supposed Katarina was feeling up to the task. Despite my reservations, I found myself walking towards her. Perhaps it was due to her overwhelming presence.

"...Sophia. I..." *I may be able to speak the lines provided for me. However, to hold another man's fiancée in these arms...*

"No, Big Brother. You must try. After all, you have already graduated from the academy, and we are at a clear disadvantage! We have to seize the opportunity and approach at this crucial moment!" Sophia spoke softly, but from her tone, I understood that no form of rebellion would be tolerated.

My sister had noticed my feelings long ago. She had sincerely cheered me on, hoping that Katarina and I would develop a deeper bond... but I always knew it was impossible. I did not want to snatch her away from Jeord. However, if we grew too close... perhaps, my desires would only grow.

Even with those thoughts in mind... I felt myself unable to resist Sophia's determined, expectant eyes. I steeled myself. "Are you ready, Katarina?" I asked for one final confirmation.

Katarina simply answered me cheerfully. "Yes. I shall do my best to be your partner in this endeavor, Master Nicol, for Sophia's sake! You can count on me."

"Is that so...? Thank you." Katarina was so gentle and straightforward. I felt a hint of happiness wash over me as I looked upon her face. Those aqua-blue eyes, staring straight at me. *Ah... I truly love this girl.*

"I love you."

The words from my lips were merely a line from a play. Or were they words from my heart...? Katarina was to respond with her lines next. *"Me too, my prince,"* she would say.

"...M-Me... too. Master Nicol," she said, with slightly reddened cheeks.

In that moment, my mind was blank. And then... I felt a burning sensation, heat, rising up from deep within me. She had answered to my line. *"I love you,"* I'd said. And yet, she answered with my name. I was filled with a sense of bliss that I had never felt before.

What little remained of my rationality sought to advise Katarina on her erroneous delivery of her lines. But... it was a lie. The thought of me not wanting to snatch her from Jeord's arms... was a lie. I had lied to myself. I had desperately tried to contain my feelings.

In truth, I wanted to be with her. I desired the girl known as Katarina Claes, so much so that it felt like my heart would rend in two. I wanted to snatch her from Jeord's arms. I wanted to make her my own. The mental cage that I had locked my feelings in... I could feel it shaking, rattling.

"Um... Master Nicol..." Once more, she spoke my name from those lips. I could no longer hold back. With a swift motion, I held her soft, warm body cin my arms.

"...Katarina. Even if you belong to someone else... I... will certainly..." *I will certainly never give up on you. Not for all eternity. Never.*

And then... what will come of it? When one day... I can no longer hold back these feelings?

★★★★★★★★★★

A school festival was being held at the Academy of Magic, the school that I had belonged to just last year. I had joined as a first-year student, and I was a member of the council back then. However... my only memories of the festival during that year were that of us dealing with the troubles surrounding one of my classmates, Nicol Ascart. I could not remember anything else.

Two years had passed since then. I had gone by the name of Sirius at the time. The Magical Ministry had taken me in ever since, and I now went by Raphael Wolt — my real name.

Today, as part of my tasks at the Ministry, I was to attend a school festival at the Academy of Magic once again. It was a small area of the festival, really — a display space showcasing works by students, with some of these works being sold. The Ministry would have some items on sale as well, and managing that was part of my job.

Nearby was none other than Maria Campbell, with her small display of what seemed to be homemade snacks. Just the previous year, I had been in the council, just like she was. Although I had given her some painful memories and caused her no end of trouble during the incident the previous year, Maria had been astonishingly forgiving, and had accepted my apology most graciously. She said these words with the kindest of smiles: "From now on, please live — as your real self."

Up until then, I had been irritated by the constant monologues of a certain young girl, claiming that "Ah, Maria was really an angel!" and "Maria... my goddess." When she said those words to me, however, it felt like she was indeed an angel. If I had been anyone but myself, perhaps I, too, would have fallen for Maria.

However... I had fallen for *her* — before Maria. Her brown hair, whipped up by the winds... my eyes locked onto her form almost immediately. The girl illuminated her surroundings just by being there.

"Lady Katarina, it's been a while." At my words, the girl I had fallen head over heels for, Katarina Claes, opened her azure eyes wide in surprise.

"Raphael! You're participating in the festival too?"

"Yes. I am in charge of curating the items presented for sale at the festival, you see."

I had deliberately altered my appearance after those events. Having retrieved my real name, and now leading a new life, this had been necessary so that I wouldn't stand out as much. Hardly anyone expressed interest towards me in this form. It was as if I had become someone else altogether.

Even so, Katarina immediately noticed me. And then, with that usual, straightforward gaze of hers... she turned to me.

85

I had done something unspeakable to Katarina. I wouldn't have been surprised if she never wanted anything to do with me again. And yet... Katarina smiled gently, just as she always did. Nothing had changed.

"I see you're working hard!"

"Yes. I am at the bottom of the food chain, after all, and there is much work to be done." However... I couldn't be any happier than I was right now. The stagnant sense of anger and hatred within me had long since faded. I no longer lived a falsified existence.

I was truly blessed to be able to once again hold that happiness, happiness which I thought I'd lost back in the days of my childhood. Up until last year, when Katarina had reached her hand out to me, I could have never dreamed that I would be able to live such blissful days. Such thoughts were nothing more than dreams to me.

Although the Ministry's research facility stood on the same grounds as the Academy of Magic, we each had our lives to live. I had work to handle at the Ministry, and Katarina and her friends had lessons to take. We couldn't find the time in our busy lives to meet often. This was why I was glad that we were able to see each other on this day, for the first time in a long time.

I listened to Katarina's situation and spoke a little of mine. I was able to speak with her for a while — it wasn't long before Maria noticed us, however, and she soon walked towards us. She greeted Katarina and handed her a pack of snacks that seemed to be the same kind she'd been selling at her stand.

"Wow! Thank you for setting some aside for me! How were the sales?" Katarina inquired, happily accepting the snacks.

"Of course, Lady Katarina. Honestly... I was worried, thinking that the snacks I made would not sell at all. But thanks to you, Lady

Katarina, I am almost completely sold out." Maria, too, seemed very pleased.

Honestly, I had my doubts about the snacks selling upon hearing that they were homemade by Maria, since she was the only commoner in the academy. All the other students were of noble origin. Nobles, of course, did not cook their own meals, and all of their food was prepared by trained chefs and staff. Would they be willing to taste food prepared by an amateur? I pondered on these points silently at the time.

It would seem that Katarina was the one who was behind it. As usual, I found myself surprised at her sudden, inexplicable ideas and decisions. For example, I was surprised when she had asked to taste Maria's baked goods last year, back when we were all in the council. While I had been born a commoner, and did recall tasting some of the snacks my mother baked back when I was a child, Katarina was different. She was born a noble — and the daughter of a duke, of all things. I had assumed that she would simply be fed high-class, haute cuisine food on a regular basis. Why would she of all people ask to taste the baked goods that Maria, a commoner, made?

At first, I'd thought that Katarina was simply being sympathetic to the challenges Maria faced in the academy. It would seem that I was mistaken, however. She really did want to taste Maria's homemade snacks. And so Maria delivered on Katarina's desires. Unexpectedly, her baked goods tasted respectable — much more so than the work of a typical patisserie. They were truly delicious.

Ever since, Katarina continued asking for Maria's snacks, and before long the two had become quite close. Nobles tended to be haughty and arrogant simply because of their position and social standing. It was not uncommon for them to look down on others.

Katarina, however, did not have a fragment of that in her soul. Never once did she attempt to approach the princes near her with untoward advances, nor did she look down on the commoner Maria. It was almost as if she herself did not think very much of her social standing as a noble.

While Katarina felt this way, however, some other students did not necessarily share her sentiments. This was why I had been worried about the whole affair — would Maria's snacks sell...? But by the time I had thought to look, Maria's little display stand was almost empty, with only one or two packs left. She was almost sold out.

Even Katarina seemed surprised at this development. "They must have been popular! Of course, since they're your homemade snacks, Maria."

"No, this is thanks to your assistance as well, Lady Katarina. After all, you spread the word far and wide, didn't you?" Katarina's advertising attempts seemed to have successfully spread the word amongst the student base.

However, looking at Maria, I didn't feel like that was the entire reason. Although she seemed a little detached and uncomfortable when she had just enrolled, being amongst a crowd of nobles, it would seem that she had already become somewhat used to the academy. Noble girls who had kept their distance from Maria in the past now comfortably approached her full of smiles, talking to her and purchasing her snacks. Her features, which used to be clouded by a myriad of suppressed emotions, had now softened, and her smile calming and kind. This, too, must have been due to Katarina's influence.

"Well, I did advertise. But the snacks wouldn't have sold like this if they weren't so delicious! The reason they're so popular is because they taste good!"

The color in Maria's cheeks deepened noticeably as she happily listened to Katarina's shower of praise and thanked her for it. Maria Campbell had certainly fallen for Katarina as well, much like I had. This was why... she must have already made a decision.

"Come to think of it, Lady Campbell has decided to sign up at the Ministry, or so I hear..." Talk had come up recently of Maria joining the ranks of the Ministry. In fact, she had received recommendations ever since she had enrolled into the academy — recently, my workplace had been ablaze with talk of Maria's recruitment.

Maria confirmed this, and Katarina reacted with surprise, pointing out that she had said that she wanted to return home and live quietly after graduation. In fact, I did recall Maria saying something like that to me once before.

"Well... It is true, that was what I had thought shortly after enrolling in the academy, that I would simply return home and live a quiet life... but..." Maria said, her gaze focused and determined. "If I did that, then I could no longer be by your side."

"Hm?" Katarina simply stood still for a while, as if not understanding the significance of Maria's words. I, however, understood it well enough. After all, I had those exact same feelings as well.

"Just like I asked during the graduation ceremony last year, Lady Katarina, I would like to stay by your side. However... even if I am a Wielder of Light, I am but a commoner. I need a certain degree of social standing to stand by you — given that you are a noble, and the daughter of Duke Claes. And so I decided that I would join the Ministry, and attain the position I require."

Maria's words, much like a passionate confession of love, succeeded in turning Katarina's cheeks bright red. It didn't take long for Maria to notice Katarina blushing at her words, which simply served to intensify the deepening shade of red across her own features. Katarina and Maria, facing each other with embarrassed, reddened faces.

I wanted to join in on the conversation as well, but it was like the two of them had created a world of their own. I did not find this amusing in the slightest. In fact, did these two girls forget that I was still here?

"Ah... do excuse me. I hate to interrupt the private world that the two of you have conjured... but I am present as well... yes?" Being left behind and forgotten in this fashion was far too cruel for me to bear.

"Ah... oh, Raphael. A private world, you say...?" At last, Katarina was looking in my direction. Maria was still somewhat red-faced, but at last, I was now within her field of vision once more.

"To think that the motivation for you joining the Ministry, the apple of this kingdom's eye... is to be with Lady Katarina. As expected of you, Lady Campbell."

The Magical Ministry was the largest association in the kingdom. It wielded the most power, coming only after the king. As such, many staff members signed up with suitably lofty aims and noble goals, such as "the advancement and evolution of magic and magecraft." Maria's reasons for joining up with the Ministry, however, were a little different.

"I do understand that my reasons for joining the Ministry may be... improper. But even so, I intend to give it my all once I join its ranks. I will be in your care," Maria replied with no hint of hesitation.

I understood her reasons all too well. Yet I had to point out that even if she did join the Ministry, Katarina would be marrying Prince Jeord after graduation, and would become so busy that we would no longer be able to see her often.

It would seem that Maria hadn't been aware of the situation from this angle — her eyes were opened wide in surprise. Despite her steadfast nature, she seemed to occasionally overlook the strangest things. But then, even Katarina herself was surprised. Their surprise was contagious, and soon I felt taken aback as well.

Maria being surprised is one thing... but Katarina's the one getting married, here! Judging by Katarina's stunned expression, I suppose she's more airheaded than I'd originally imagined... but for it to be this extreme...?

"That... That's right... Lady Katarina is Prince Jeord's fiancée... She will immediately become his bride after graduation, and spend her days in the castle. We may not be able to see her then. I don't think I would like that very much..."

"Yes... if this goes on, I have to marry Jeord and become a royal. That would be bad... I'm barely making it as the daughter of a duke, but a royal...!"

Given that Katarina herself was so well-loved and pampered by her fiancé, Prince Jeord, it was without question that she would simply be spirited away for the marriage eventually. In fact, given that it was Jeord, she may very well be taken into the depths of the royal castle and never see the light of day again. A terrifying prospect.

Katarina, being dense as she was, however, did not appear to have noticed Jeord's feelings for her at all. And she had described her situation in quite the dire fashion; she didn't seem keen on the idea of marrying and becoming royalty.

I offered some words of assistance to the shaken Katarina and Maria. In fact, I had brought up the subject of Maria joining the Ministry all for it to lead up to this moment.

"...Have you considered joining the Ministry as well, Lady Katarina?"

Katarina, shaken as she was, was immediately attracted by my words. "Huh? I can do that? Actually, does joining the Ministry mean I wouldn't have to get married anymore?"

"Basically, it is possible for one to join the ranks of the Ministry with the recommendation of a staff member with considerable social standing. While I do not think that simply joining the Ministry would cancel the entire engagement, the Ministry is only second to the king himself when it comes to political power. I hardly think that you would be dragged off to the castle immediately."

In truth, I had been thinking about this subject for quite a while. *What is the best way I can go about this? How can I prevent Katarina from immediately falling into Jeord's arms after her graduation?* After all, I had planned and plotted for a long, long time. Although I had not done so out of my own free will, I had become surprisingly good at it. Upon hearing talk of Maria's imminent recruitment into the Ministry's ranks... I decided to get Maria on my side.

As expected, Maria's eyes, too, were sparkling with expectation — she was attentively listening to every single word. However, Katarina, who seemed visibly interested at first, now had a somewhat clouded expression. "Um... Raphael. As you may know, my magical capability is... depressingly low..."

"Ah, about that. While it is indeed true that there are many in the Ministry who have high magical capability, there are equally many who are not as magically gifted. After all, we do not exactly turn away those who are simply interested in magic."

What I said was true. There were many people in the Ministry who were talented at magic, but not everyone was that way. After all, having a high magical capability and aptitude did not mean that one was necessarily intelligent. Amongst the researchers, there were actually fewer individuals with high magical capability.

"Is that so?! That's great! Well then, I'll do my best. But didn't you say that I needed a letter of recommendation from an important person in the Ministry? Ugh... Then this will be really difficult, won't it? After all, no one would give someone like me a recommendation..."

The Magical Ministry was a unique organization. Although elites and capable individuals were gathered annually to go through an acceptance test, few made it into the Ministry via this path. The reason for this was simple — those who wielded particularly strong magic, like Maria, were often spoken to at some point during their time at the academy. And those without magic relied on connections instead, or were genuinely recommended by current members of staff.

Furthermore, it wasn't possible for just any staff member to write letters of recommendation. I myself was on the lowest rung in the Ministry, so my word would not count for much. However.

"Don't be so sad, Lady Katarina. There is in fact... someone who would write a letter of recommendation for you."

With that, I described how my superior had become interested in her, and would surely write her the letter she needed. The face of my superior — a woman known for her eccentricity, momentarily flashed through my mind.

When it was time to decide how the affair of my affiliation would be handled, most staff members at the Ministry held their peace. But of course they would; who would want to take in a criminal, a member of a Marquess family, and someone who had wielded forbidden, taboo Dark Magic? No one had wanted to dirty their hands by taking in someone like that. No one... except...

"What, no department wants him? Really? A rare guy like him? How wonderful. Well then, my colleagues. If none of you would like

him, I'll have him." Saying so, she took me in, all the while with that charming, seductive smile on their face. This was how I ended up in my current situation.

I was not treated as a special case of any sort, and was working hard just like any other member of the Magical Ministry. In fact, my boss was the person who had taught me how to disguise myself and alter my appearance.

I was surprised that she would know about Katarina at all. Once, I had coincidentally met with Katarina on the grounds. After a casual conversation with her, I returned, only to be cornered and practically interrogated. "*Are you familiar with Katarina Claes, by any chance...?*"

For some reason, my boss was very interested in meeting with Katarina. "*Where did you meet her? Come now. You simply must tell me,*" she said. Ever since then, my boss had been pleased by my tales and stories of Katarina Claes, but it would seem that she now wished to speak to her in person. Given that she had this much interest in Katarina, surely she would have no issues providing her with a letter of recommendation.

Katarina asked what kind of person she was, and I described her as an individualistic, but kind person. In fact, Katarina, being strange as she was, may very well get along well with that boss of mine.

"Um, excuse me!" Maria said, interrupting the conversation somewhat forcibly. She had a desperate expression on her face. "U-Um. Well... if we were to summarize what we've just learned... if Raphael's superior would indeed write you a letter of recommendation, and you enter the Magical Ministry... then... then! Then we would be together forever!"

Maria's reaction lined up well with my predictions. "That would be so, yes," I said, giving the desperate Maria a gentle smile — and she returned the gesture, genuine happiness lighting up her face.

"Lady Katarina, let's join the ranks of the Ministry together. I will do what I can to help! Please, you must, oh you must!" Maria said, holding Katarina's hands as her eyes sparkled.

Yes... things are smoothly progressing according to plan. With this, Maria was now my ally, and Katarina had set her sights upon working at the Ministry... with this, we would be together next year as well.

While I do apologize for using you in this fashion, Maria... I really do not want to hand Katarina off to Jeord. I would like her to stay by my side for just a little while longer.

★★★★★★★★★

A fountain shot up like a geyser from the central pool, and the falling droplets of water formed a rainbow. Earthen sculptures changed their shape over and over as people watched on. Around them were vibrant wreaths of flame. A small tornado of wind whipped up flower petals into the air.

Standing next to this ethereal scene, all I could do was face the endless stream of crowds and visitors with a forced smile. This wasn't just a party that lasted for a few hours or some ball. I couldn't keep this irritating smile on my face the whole day!

But next to me was my twin brother, Jeord, with his usual flawless smile on his face. Naturally, since he's quite the capable guy.

I'm Alan Stuart, and was born with my twin sixteen years ago. When we were younger, Jeord always did the best at everything so effortlessly, all with that smug face of his. I couldn't help but feel inferior to him.

But during that time, I met that strange noble girl. She was the daughter of a duke, and yet she'd hike up her skirt, run everywhere, and climb up trees like some kind of monkey. I'd never met anyone like that before. Katarina Claes… a kid who broke all the rules when it came to how noble girls should act.

She taught me one thing, though. That everyone was different, and everyone had their own unique strengths. Once I understood that, I could finally relax. The tension faded from my shoulders as my inferiority complex towards Jeord vanished.

After that… for some reason, I always wanted to be around Katarina. Why? Because it was peaceful. It felt good. All I wanted to do was spend more time with her, but… as the years went by, I started to feel my heartbeat speeding up and my face turning red if she brushed against me or anything like that.

Just when I was wondering what that was all about… *that* happened. Katarina was nearly killed. It was only then that I noticed my own feelings for the first time. I had fallen in love with my brother's fiancée, of all people.

It's not like I can just walk in and take his fiancée away. If it was just some kind of political marriage and the two of them didn't care for each other, then that would be one thing. But just look at the guy. Even I get embarrassed just watching Jeord go love crazy when he's around her. Though Katarina, for some reason, never seems to notice.

And then there's the fact that I have a fiancée of my own; Mary Hunt, the daughter of Marquess Hunt. Wise and beautiful, she's the very image of a noble lady. I feel like a girl like that was wasted on me. I like her, and want to cherish her forever… but it isn't love. It's more like how a brother might feel for a sister. I realized the difference once I noticed my feelings for Katarina.

Once I understood all this, I went to speak with Mary. I was planning on canceling our engagement, since I was in love with someone else. Of course, I couldn't just go and say "Oh, that someone else is my brother's fiancée," so I just told her it was "forbidden love."

Then, Mary said that she herself felt the same way. She had feelings for someone else, and it was also a kind of forbidden love. We talked about it for a while, and she decided that she wanted to stick with the current arrangement. After all, she'd just be engaged to someone else if we called it off. I agreed with her suggestion, and so our engagement is still on.

Who is this forbidden person that Mary loved so much? I have no idea. She said she'd never give up, though. I promised her that I'd call the engagement off if she ever managed to reach a conclusion with the person she loved.

As we both cheered each other on, I found myself getting closer to Mary. It was under her request that I started keeping an eye on Jeord's movements and telling her everything he did. Katarina was a dear friend, and we didn't want Jeord to have her all to himself.

I felt like I was exploiting Mary's pure feelings. I didn't feel good about it, but... honestly? Keeping Jeord and Katarina's bond from deepening any further was a good thing for me, so I gladly cooperated with her.

I was keeping an eye on Jeord today too. Mary had asked me to make sure that he didn't end up alone with Katarina. *It's a request from my fiancée, after all.* With that reason in mind, I decided to get in Jeord's way as much as I could. I'm not the type who's good at giving up.

I was spending so much time thinking about the situation with Mary that I hadn't noticed that Katarina had showed up until she was already next to Jeord. They seemed to be talking happily. *They really get along well, huh?* But Mary asked me to be on Jeord's tail, so I walked towards them, planning on disrupting their meeting.

"Oh, it's you two. So you're finally here? Thought you wouldn't make it, see. After you said all that about 'I'll come by with gifts!' this morning too… thought you wouldn't get here, being so late and all," I said as I approached them.

"I apologize… A bunch of things slowed me down along the way."

"That right? I figured you ended up eating endlessly at the stands and forgot all about the time."

"…" Katarina's expression became rigid. Guess I hit the nail on the head. *Katarina… you're as easy to read as ever.*

"Here, for you. Please try them." Obviously trying to change the subject, Katarina withdrew something from her bag and gave it to me. From what I could see, it was a pack of snacks, the same kind that another member of the student council, Maria, made.

Jeord asked about how well the snacks had sold, and Katarina responded joyously. "Yes, they were very popular. In fact, they'd almost sold out by the time I got there." She was so glad, talking like she was the one who had sold all the snacks.

"Is that so? That is good to hear, Katarina," Jeord responded. But then Katarina seemed to be thinking about something. She didn't respond, even when I called out to her. She was lost in her own world.

"…Again, Katarina…?" Jeord asked, obviously exasperated. Sometimes, she would forget all about her surroundings and just stand there, unable to hear a thing. This was one of those times.

"Hey, Katarina Claes! Lady Dimwit! No good... she isn't listening at all." I tried calling out to her once more, with a slightly louder voice this time, but she didn't say a thing. It was obvious that talking to her was pointless now. With that, I lightly rapped her head with a free hand.

"Wh-What are you doing?!" I didn't even use that much force, but Katarina seemed extremely surprised, staring at me with narrowed eyes.

"Your fault for not listening when people are talking to you," I said. It was true.

"Th-Then all you had to do was say something! You didn't have to rap me on the head!"

She's got a lot of nerve being the offended one here! I guess she really didn't hear anything. "What are you blathering about, dummy? I did that already! It's your fault for not reacting at all."

With that, Katarina started pouting, vocalizing her annoyance. *Ugh... The way her eyes slant upward when she pouts like that... is kind of cute too. But I won't be shaken.* I immediately started to mess with her hair.

"That is quite enough, Alan. I would strongly prefer that you do not touch her so casually." Jeord's hand was now firmly around my arm. He was smiling as always... but his eyes were not.

"...Ahh, Jeord... you're always like this," I sighed in spite of myself. This twin brother of mine was usually relaxed and carefree... but when it came to Katarina, his emotions always floated up to the surface like this.

I had barely touched her, and yet Jeord was staring daggers at me, as if he was ready to kill me if I went any further. *Geez, what a pain.* I would have loved to go back in time and show Jeord's

99

expression to my past self, back when I'd thought he was perfect in every way.

Not only was Jeord Stuart a lovestruck fool for his fiancée, he was also way too uptight. Even Mary, my own fiancée, had this to say: *"If he were to restrict Lady Katarina in such a way... it would only provoke those around him to look upon him with distaste. And sooner or later... Lady Katarina herself will be tired of him."*

"Aren't you being a little too uptight? Keep that up and you're going to be disliked eventually... That's what Mary says."

"Do inform Lady Mary that her concern is most misplaced." His response was cold. His eyes were cold. *Gah... this guy's impossible. Lovesick fool.*

Also... he's being a little too hard on my arm, yeah? All I did was touch her head a little bit. Look at him, hugging and touching Katarina all day. And that's okay? What a stingy guy. Just as I was about to give Jeord a well-placed retort of my own out of sheer irritation...

"Jeord, Alan." I heard voices call out from behind us. I turned and saw that two couples were walking towards us, with the man in front smiling.

Gah...! Someone even more irritating than Jeord is here...

It was Jeffrey Stuart, our oldest brother. He shook both our hands with a really annoying expression. A little behind Jeffrey was Ian, our other older brother. He was the direct opposite of Jeffrey, always with a serious expression. He bowed slightly.

Ever since coming to the academy, I hadn't seen my brothers much at all. Even though we lived in the same place growing up, the two of them were always busy fighting over the throne. They hardly spoke to their younger brothers at all, or even had anything to do with us. We weren't very close.

Before I went to the academy, I would occasionally run into them at the palace. I never knew how to deal with them. Especially our oldest brother, Jeffrey...

"Oh, if it isn't Lady Katarina Claes. Long time no see," Jeffrey said to Katarina, in a most casual and carefree manner that wasn't prince-like at all.

Yeah... she met him once. She met them both, actually, during Jeord's and my fifteenth birthday party. Judging from her expression, though, she probably didn't remember them at all. Jeord, who had been watching the entire time, quickly whispered bits of information into her ear.

"Ah, yes. It has... been quite a while indeed, Prince Jeffrey, Prince Ian..." With that, Katarina went quiet. If she didn't remember my brothers, then she definitely wouldn't remember their fiancées. Jeord started subtly whispering again.

"It's good to see you Lady Randall, Lady Berg." Jeord had unmistakably just reminded her of their names... but Katarina greeted them naturally, as if she had known of them the entire time. My brother's fiancées, in turn, greeted her as well.

"What brings you to this place today, brothers?" Jeord asked.

Jeffrey was the one who answered. "Why, to witness my beloved little brothers' amazing exhibition, of course!"

Ah... this brother of ours. He'll never change. Jeffrey had always been like this. The rumors were one thing, but I honestly had no idea whether he was all there. He always acted like a normal person at official functions and stuff, but he was carefree and casual the rest of the time, always saying stupid things with that irritating face.

Naturally, Jeord knew this all too well. "So... how about we come clean, Ian?" Ignoring Jeffrey altogether, he instead turned to Ian for answers.

"Of course. We are here on royal business. A routine examination… inspection of the Academy of Magic. I suppose Jeffrey is here on similar grounds as well." Ian was the same as always too. He was serious and rigid, and that's about it.

"You suppose? Ah. I see that you two have not arrived together."

"It goes without saying. We had just crossed paths with each other, coincidentally, moments ago."

Jeffrey and Ian were always fighting over the throne… so, you know. They're not often found together, or seen together at all. Even so, looking at them now, the two seemed to get along okay. They weren't at each other's throats, anyway.

But I knew that each of them had their own political factions to answer to, so I supposed they couldn't be too friendly with all those eyes around them watching.

Before I knew it, Jeffrey, who had been collectively ignored by both Jeord and Ian, now turned his eyes on me. *Ugh, this is definitely bad.*

"Huh? You're both no fun, Jeord, Ian! Well then… come here, Alan! Big Brother is here to see you!"

"H-Hey! Stop it. Don't hug me." I was now firmly in Jeffrey's embrace. To be held by a man, even if he was my brother, was just too weird at my age. I struggled against Jeffrey's arms.

Just as all this was happening, the chiming of bells rang out from overhead. *Clang! Clang!*

Guess there's not much time left in this whole school festival deal… Time had passed quickly while I wasn't paying attention. In just a short while, the festival would end and then we would be moving on to the night event, which was a ball.

"Ah. Do excuse us. We have to head to the stage soon," Jeord said as the bells rang out. We did have a performance by the council planned and all that, after all.

Honestly… acting really wasn't my thing. But the student body strongly requested it, so I had no choice but to participate.

"Ohh? A performance, Jeord? I would like to see it too, oh yes."

Ian was quick to reprimand Jeffrey for his flippant lines. "Enough with the tomfoolery, Jeffrey. We're heading back."

"Whaaa…? You really are no fun, Ian. Actually, Ian… you're heading back with me?"

"As I said, enough nonsense. There is no way I could return with you."

The same banter as always, I guess. Our talkative, flippant, somewhat annoying oldest brother… the always-serious, ever so formal second brother. Even though I didn't spend much time with them, and actually didn't like dealing with them, I couldn't bring myself to hate them or anything. But yeah… I'd still balk at the idea of meeting these two again.

"See ya!"

"Well then. Do excuse us."

With their contrasting goodbyes, our older brothers were gone, and we headed to the stage. I couldn't help but notice that there was still a bag in Katarina's hands. There was still so much food in it. *Isn't she done giving out her gifts? Don't tell me… all that in there is for her to eat by herself…?*

Well… whatever. Guess I'll tell Mary about how I didn't let Jeord spend any significant amount of time with Katarina alone…

★★★★★★★★★

The school festival would be coming to an end shortly. *Honestly, what a boring, tiresome day.* Because I was so bogged down with work — not only today, but also ever since we began festival preparations — I had been unable to spend any meaningful time with Katarina. I found myself quite irritated.

To make matters worse, I had invited Katarina to my quarters just before my schedule had become incredibly busy — but of course, Keith was there, getting in our way as usual. I decided that then I could pay her a visit, only for Mary and Alan to obstruct me at every turn. Although Katarina was engaged to me, Jeord Stuart, it would seem that all of these other fools had no intention of giving up.

My fiancée, Katarina Claes, was… different. She was not at all what a noble lady… well, rather, she was unlike any normal girl at all. By her side, I was never bored. No matter how many years I spent with her, every moment was unfailingly vibrant and wonderful.

Originally, I had little interest in the affairs of others. I had never thought it possible that I would feel such affection for another. The one who had taught me I could feel this way was, of course, Katarina herself.

Even so… her charm was her downfall. After all, this naturally meant that my rivals would increase in number. Katarina was quite the charmer, you see, although she herself was not aware of it. To make things worse, her sheer lovability drew both men and women to her.

First to fall was her adopted brother, then my younger brother and his fiancée, and then there was my childhood friend, the chancellor's son, and his younger sister. After that was a Wielder of Light who was a genius of a girl in her own right. Finally, even the individual who had made an attempt on her life ended up falling for her as well. The number of rivals I had to deal with simply kept increasing.

Even today, Katarina arrived late. Distracted by the food offerings at the stands, perhaps. And just when we were having a private conversation, Alan showed up to get in my way. To make things worse... he so casually touched her head.

Katarina is mine. You would do well to keep your hands off her. As soon as I reprimanded Alan for his actions, he called me "uptight."

Well. Perhaps he did have a point, at least when it came to Katarina. Although I was usually calm and hardly shaken by anything, I felt my tolerance narrow significantly when it came to anything that involved her.

Honestly... seeing Katarina speak to other men alone was enough to fill me with displeasure. But then again, with so many enemies in my presence, I supposed there was little I could do about it.

And then there was the constant worrying — wondering if Katarina had unknowingly ended up charming someone else without realizing it again. Although she had finally made her way here, we hardly had any time to speak, and soon we already had to make our way to the stage venue. I remained in a considerably bad mood.

To think that when I had finally had some time with her, not only Alan, but also my older brothers had showed up. Their timing could not possibly have been any worse. Of all the times they could have come, why pick the moment when I could have been alone with Katarina? There had been so much pointless, wasted time before all this. Why not then? Why now? There would have been no issues if they had arrived just a little earlier.

Leaving the stoic and strict Ian aside... I found it difficult to deal with that flippant sod of a brother of ours, Jeffrey. But of course, I was hardly like Alan — such emotions did not show on my face.

Although I was able to easily read the thoughts and machinations of most individuals, my oldest brother was an exception. I had been unable to read him ever since our younger days together. He was a little disturbing, if anything. I could never quite understand what he was thinking at any given point in time. Even so, he clearly did not have any intention of hurting us, so I supposed that thought could be shelved.

Thanks to the pointless formalities of our older brothers, it was already somewhat late by the time we reached the venue. The other members of the student council had already gathered. Some of the female students had already changed into their costumes. It was time for me to make preparations as well, but...

"It's terrible! One of the actresses is unwell, and can no longer perform!" one of the backstage assistants said, running towards us. It would seem like a certain first year, who was one of the actresses in the production, had suddenly collapsed. She was brought to the infirmary.

Thankfully, her diagnosis was positive; all the girl needed was a bit of rest, and she would recover in due time. However, there was no way an ailing girl could participate in the production, especially not when it was about to start.

I inwardly sighed. *What is this production coming to, with all these last-minute occurrences?* "We have no choice. We will simply have to find a replacement."

I turned to the other students tasked with helping out backstage. They had witnessed our practice sessions many times — we would simply have to find a replacement from within their number. The students, however, all averted their gazes. But of course they would, given that they had just been suddenly called upon to stand on stage.

Compounding the situation was the fact that most of the actors and actresses selected for the performance were wildly popular amongst the student body. A poorly-selected replacement would surely suffer from public backlash — at least, that was most likely their fear.

In that case... we must find someone who is equally popular. Someone who would be a worthy replacement. Naturally, I moved my eyes to her, only for her to dramatically avert her gaze.

It was... far too obvious. Those around her had done so with a more refined sense of subtlety, but of course, she had no such tact. My voice was not the one that first called out to her, however. Instead, it was a slowly rising wave of murmurs, each voicing their approval.

"Well then... in that case, wouldn't Lady Katarina be fit for the role?" A single voice echoed through the silent backstage area.

One after another, more voices of approval sprung up from the crowd. Well... this was the natural conclusion. Anyone would have reached it with some degree of thought. Although Katarina herself was not part of the council, she was quite popular indeed, and was perhaps the only student not in the student council to have an unofficial fan following.

"I... I c-can't..." Katarina said, desperately refusing the role. She looked towards me with pleading eyes, as if asking for me to side with her. Her pleading, almost teary-eyed look was lovable too.

I smiled, ever so slightly, in response. "Well then, Katarina. I leave it in your capable hands," I said, placing a hand reassuringly on her shoulder as I did so. Katarina's expression, however, almost seemed to suggest that the world itself was about to end.

After quite some dallying, Katarina finally accepted her lines and headed off to get changed. As luck would have it, the girl who had collapsed earlier was about the same size and build as Katarina, and so the costume fit her just fine.

However... Perhaps no one had noticed it when the original actress had tried it on, but Katarina's costume was a little too revealing around the chest region. I did not like the thought of her parading in front of the crowd while dressed like that. But there was no time to change the costume.

In the end, I had the students in charge of stage costumes remedy the problem with a well-placed stole. While the students who helped her into the outfit did raise some objections, "Um... I don't think that this really fits together," I silenced them with a single look.

Katarina, however, seemed to think that the costume was meant to be this way.

With that, Katarina was finally standing near the stage curtains. The role that she would play was that of the protagonist's mean-spirited stepsister, who would bully and mock her. It was a role not particularly well-suited to Katarina... but we had no choice.

Honestly speaking, I would have much preferred for Katarina to be cast as the protagonist, who would be partnered with me in the production. That would have pleased me greatly. However, that would be much too sudden; given that Katarina was already so overwhelmed with a role that had so few lines, it would have been too much to ask of her.

Maria, playing the role of the protagonist, was already standing on the stage. Soon it would be Katarina's turn. Up until a few moments ago, Katarina had been desperately writing on something in the palm of her hand. She then brought it close to her lips. This strange series of actions would repeat several times before she ran out to the stage in a panic.

And then... Katarina froze immediately after she had made her stage debut. *Ah... could it be? Perhaps she has forgotten her lines.* Although she had practiced them several times, she hadn't had any time for them to sink in, after all.

Perhaps having Katarina act was a little too much to ask for in the first place, given that she usually lived with her heart on her sleeve. I had, of course, prepared for such an event... and just as I was about to move to support her—

"Honestly. Do you really not know your place?" A voice could be clearly heard from the direction of the stage.

There was no such line in our scripts. Surprised, I turned my eyes to the stage, only to see Katarina — although she was... different. It was as if she had the face of another person altogether.

Honestly... acting aside, I had thought that it would be all but impossible for Katarina, of all people, to take on a role that involved bullying and hurting others. I felt this way on the basis that I knew her well. I had thought that she would surely not be suited for the role...

On the stage stood a girl that was Katarina, and yet at the same time not her in the slightest. With those upwards-slanting eyes, mean smile, and intimidating expression, I could not see this girl as anyone but the protagonist's abusive stepsister.

So Katarina was capable of acting after all... I had thought that nine years was more than enough to experience all the surprises she had to offer, but it appeared I was mistaken. I should have known better than to think I would ever be able to predict anything about Katarina.

"Someone like you should just lie down in the dirt and stay there. After all, that suits you best." Those were not lines in the script by any means. Katarina, however, delivered those lines most naturally. Before I knew it... I was unable to take my eyes off her.

Standing on the stage... was a Katarina I did not yet know.

Although I could not help but be charmed by Katarina's performance, I finished my part in the production without any problems.

I was not the only one who had been entranced. As soon as the play ended, Katarina was immediately surrounded by admirers. *Ahh... seeing a side of Katarina I did not yet know was a joy indeed, but with this, she will gain even more secret admirers.*

Perhaps exposing Katarina to the masses in this fashion was a mistake. Now bathed in regret, I somehow managed to part the crowds and made it to Katarina's side, showering her with praise... and intimidating those around her in the process.

"It would be an honor to escort you to the ball, Katarina... my dear fiancée." Although I received several glares from other student council members, the fact remained that Katarina was engaged to me. As her escort for the ball, I simply refused to allow any of them to get in my way.

After all... I had been unable to speak with Katarina properly all day. I wanted to ensure that we would thoroughly enjoy our time together that night. At the ball, I would be able to hold Katarina close to me — as close as I wanted, for as long as I wanted. She would simply think that the pointed stares around her were normal, and would leave the dancing all to me.

From what I understood, my other rivals would most likely invite her to dance as well — but today was an exception. I would not hand her over so easily. Ever since I had come across that hidden side of Katarina at the performance prior, I could only feel my body heating up, my heartbeat rapidly increasing. There was no sign of it slowing down.

I would like to enjoy my time together with Katarina at the ball... enjoy it to my heart's content. Wrapping up the final bits of work I had now that the festival was at its end, I could not help but think about the time when I would have Katarina all alone to myself at the ball. *Ahh... how I wish I could just finish this here and now, and head to the ball right away.*

However... when I finally made my way to the room where she should have been waiting, with my spirits high, she was nowhere to be found. Katarina was gone. No one could find her anywhere, not even when the ball started.

The last place we had seen Katarina was the stage. We had no idea she would suddenly disappear from our sight... just like that.

An unfamiliar ceiling greeted me as I opened my eyes. I sat up slowly, inspecting my surroundings. I was in a room about the size of the one in my dormitory. The furnishings seemed expensive.

Huh...? Where's this again?

Hmm... Think, Katarina. If I recall... I had just given a great performance as a villainess, received huge amounts of praise from everyone... got really excited about that and started posing in front of the mirror in the changing room... and then someone came by and told me it was time for the ball. Huh? Then what happened after that?

Come to think of it... wasn't it nighttime? But rays of sunlight were streaming in from outside the window right now. Question after question flooded my mind — but then a knock came at the door, and a woman appeared.

She had brown hair and blue eyes, and had a sober air about her. I propped myself up on the bed, looking at her.

"Ah... I see you have awoken," she said with relief.

"Um... yes. I have." I had responded without thinking, but... who was this person again? She wasn't anyone I remembered seeing, but in my case, there was a possibility that I could have met her before and forgotten all about her.

Usually, Jeord or Keith, or anyone who was with me would help by providing me with some information. But of course, they weren't here. *I... guess I have no choice but to ask her.*

"…Um. Who… Who are you again?"

"Do excuse me. I apologize for not introducing myself. My name is Lana."

"Miss… Lana?" *Hmm… I feel like this is the first time I've met this person. That's good! That I didn't forget about someone again, I mean.*

"Please… do call me Lana. I will be taking care of your needs from today onwards, Lady Katarina."

Ah. The way she talks… is Miss Lana a maid? Come to think of it… she's wearing a complete maid uniform. Well then…

"Um… but I have a personal maid of my own. She's been with me ever since I was a child. Her name is Anne…?" I said, all the while wondering where Anne was.

Under normal circumstances, Anne would wake me and, as if she were a ninja or warrior of some kind, would quickly straighten and comb out my bed-head, preparing me for the day.

"I do apologize. That maid is… currently not here. I will be taking care of all your needs here."

"…Is that so…?" *I see… so Anne isn't here with me. That feels a little lonely… Hmm… come to think of it.* "Um… where is this, exactly?"

Maybe it was a little late for me to be asking this question, but I really didn't know where I was. To begin with… how long had I been here?

"I apologize. I am afraid I do not have the privilege of providing you with the answer to your question…" Lana said, looking troubled.

"Huh? You… can't answer me? What does that mean…?"

Lana simply continued to look upset. "If I may, Lady Katarina, perhaps you will find the answers you seek with a little more time…" Immediately after she offered her answer, another knock came from the direction of the door, and two more people appeared.

One of them was a bespectacled young man. His hair had tinges of blue to it, as did his eyes. He was quite dashing. Unlike Jeord, who looked like a traditional, fairy-tale prince, this guy was different. He oozed charisma, and seemed a bit like a playboy — at least, that was how he looked.

This playboy-like guy was wearing something that looked familiar. At Claes Manor, the only person who wore anything quite like it was an older man in our service… ah! It was a butler's uniform.

Our butler back at Claes Manor wore respectably fancy clothes as well. I secretly referred to him as "Sebastian" in my heart, even though that wasn't his name. *But… compared to this… bespectacled butler… ugh. My dear Sebastian, you have lost…*

Behind this man that our dear Sebastian had unfortunately lost to in my internal "Perfect Butler Contest" was a much smaller figure who must have been standing behind him. I had been so entranced by the butler's terribly handsome aura and had hardly noticed her at first.

I shifted my eyes to the figure. She was petite, with brown hair and large brown eyes. She looked kind of like a small, vulnerable animal. Just looking at her made you want to protect her.

I was quite forgetful and very bad with names, but even I remembered who this person was. After all, we had just met at the school festival! It was at the venue where they were showcasing the magical talents of the academy's students. She was Prince Ian's fiancée — Selena Berg. *Why is she here…? Seriously, where is this place?*

"I see you have awoken safely… Most reassuring."

Becoming increasingly confused at Selena's sudden appearance, I could only stare blankly at her face. I noticed that she had an expression of relief, much like Lana had just now. And then…

"Lady Katarina... I sincerely apologize for having to employ such uncouth means. However... as soon as the relevant affairs are settled, you will be allowed to go, unharmed... Please, do stay here until then," Selena said, bowing her head deeply.

Huh? Uncouth means? What? Why am I in such a strange, unknown place...? I desperately sifted through my memories.

That student who offered to guide me to the ball... she ended up taking a wrong turn and bringing me somewhere else. And then...? And then someone grabbed me by the arm... and suddenly shoved a cloth in my face. Hmm.

Huh? Why does this feel like the plot of a manga I read in my previous life? Come to think of it, that particular development in that one manga I read was when the main character was...

"...Kidnapped...?" I said my thoughts aloud without thinking.

Selena jumped back almost like a startled prey animal, and with an increasingly apologetic expression, bowed her head once more. "I truly... truly apologize... I promise, absolutely, that no harm would ever come to you..."

"Oh!" *Really?! I, Katarina Claes, have really been kidnapped?!* I'd thought that kidnapping and things like that only happened in manga... but now it was really happening! I was nothing more than a normal, unremarkable daughter of a salaryman back then. But now I was the daughter of Duke Claes. The risk of being kidnapped was high.

But now that the events of *Fortune Lover* were over, and I had successfully dodged all the Catastrophic Bad Ends, the possibility of being kidnapped hadn't even remotely crossed my mind. I had been celebrating ever since I had escaped all those bad endings, and had been pretty careless ever since. I really let my guard down...

115

Ahh, looking back on it, I should have listened to Keith's warnings. Anyway… just how much gold would have to be provided in exchange for my safety? I am, after all, the daughter of a duke. I suppose the ransom would be pretty high…

My father, who doted on me immensely, would certainly be willing to pay any amount of coin on short notice. What about Mother, though? If the ransom were too high… *"I suppose there's nothing we can do. We do still have Keith with us, after all… perhaps we should just give up on that foolish daughter of ours."*

That would be horrible! What if she said something like that? I couldn't bear it! Such a cold thing for a mother to say. No, Mother! You can't possibly leave me like this! I promise I won't play catch with the servants indoors anymore! I promise I won't break any more of your favorite vases, so please! I mentally pleaded with my mother. *But anyway! I have to find out just how much ransom they want for me!*

"…Um. Well then… how much would the ransom be…?" *Please, please let it be a sum that Mother would be willing to pay!*

Selena, however, simply looked even more troubled at my words. "Ran…som?"

"Yes. The amount of gold you want in exchange for my safety. How much would it be…?"

"…Ah, no. We do not have any intention of asking for a… sum of gold," Selena replied, seemingly panicked.

"Huh? It's not gold you're after? Then why did you kidnap me?" *Not… gold? Then why?* Unlike the beautiful and lovable Maria, I had the face of a villainess, my magical aptitude and capabilities were low, and I wasn't all that smart. I had assumed that all they would want from me would be the gold of the Claes family. Well, I supposed I did have enough agricultural knowledge to become a farmhand of some kind, but would these people kidnap me just for that?

"...That is..." Selena seemed to hesitate momentarily at my question. Just as she was about to answer—

"Lady Selena. You have already ascertained Lady Katarina's safety, have you not? Please, let us return to your quarters."

The dashing butler, who had been silent up until now, suddenly started talking as if panicked at what Selena was about to say. He placed a hand on her shoulder.

"Rufus... yes. Yes, let's. Well then, Lady Katarina... I shall return to my quarters..."

It would seem like the playboy-esque, seductive butler was called Rufus. *Look at him, escorting Selena like that... this is bad. I can smell the pheromones in the air.*

H-Hey! I still have things I want to ask! After all, it would feel pretty terrible to just sit here, not being able to make heads or tails of the situation. "Wha...? P-Please wait..." I tried calling out to her, but all Selena did was turn around with that same worried expression, before addressing somebody else altogether.

"I do apologize... Lana, please take care of her. Lady Katarina... if you are wanting for anything, anything at all... please inform Lana of your needs. We will aim to provide for you as best as we can."

With that, Selena disappeared, escorted away from the room by Rufus the butler. I turned my gaze to Lana, who was still in the room, and all she did was silently shake her head.

And so it came to be that I, Katarina Claes, knowing nothing about my current situation, ended up spending a strange, baffling time in an equally strange and foreign room.

★★★★★★★★★

I, Jeord Stuart, would like to think of myself as a fairly capable individual. I am able to perform most tasks with ease, and I also excel at reading the expressions of others. As such, I am able to go about most affairs without difficulty.

One of the few things I am unable to easily deal with… would be my fiancée, Katarina Claes. She first piqued my interest when we were both eight years old. Now, eight years later, I still found myself surprised by the intensity of my feelings for her. And yet, Katarina simply would not fall into my grasp. If anything, I could feel her slowly slipping further and further away, while I myself was only increasingly drawn to her the more time we spent together.

Today was no exception. I had spent eight years with her, and had thought myself to be well-acclimatized to her various habits and peculiarities. I had thought that I could no longer be surprised in any way or form. Yet the emergence of a Katarina I had never seen before on stage lit a fire in my heart. I fell for her all over again, in a whole different way.

Katarina Claes. Just how much of my heart must you take? Are you insatiable?

My increasing attraction to her felt one-sided at best. Words that would cause any other noble lady to blush hardly had any effect on Katarina. She would just stand there, unfazed, her cheeks never changing in hue. In truth, this was vexing.

This was why I had wanted to hold her close, at the very least. I wanted to feel Katarina more closely than usual at the ball. I longed to experience the softness of her skin. And yet, this dream of mine was soon shattered.

Katarina, of all people, had suddenly vanished. To make things worse, her location remained unknown as the days dragged on.

In the beginning, I had simply assumed that she had become lost somewhere in the darkened academy grounds. After all, it was no secret that she was restless, and was prone to wandering. However, it became apparent after some time that this was not the case.

To begin with… it seemed like no one had seen Katarina after she had entered the waiting room shortly after the production ended. How was that possible? In addition, there were many students who claimed to have only vague memories of that specific span of time.

I could feel dread spreading its tendrils deep into my mind as I remembered the events of last year. A forbidden, taboo magic — the Dark Arts — had been used on Katarina, and she could have very well lost her life.

However, that incident had already ended. The perpetrator, Raphael, had lost his dark powers. Then… what was it this time?! What could it be? Why Katarina, why was it always her…? My feeling of anticipation vanished almost immediately, replaced by anger and fear. We searched as hard as we could, but there were no developments. I could feel the frustration build in my mind, and then—

"…Excuse me, Prince Jeord… a letter. For you," one of my servants said, notably keeping their distance and sounding unusually reverent. I supposed even the servants were affected by how different I was from my usual self. Even I had noticed this, of course, but for some reason, I just could not bring myself to smile like I always did.

Who could it be, sending letters at this time? For the sake of my terrified servant, I made a conscious effort to soften my agitated expression. "…Who is it from?" I inquired.

The servant answered, looking troubled. "Yes, Prince Jeord... there appears to be... no declared sender."

"...You mean to say that the letter was sent anonymously?" It was common sense to include one's name on the missive, especially if it was being sent to royalty. *What is this all about? Is it some foolish noble who wishes to mock me? Or perhaps just rattle off a supposedly hurtful list of insults?* As those questions came to mind, I calmly retrieved the letter from my servant.

"I have not read the letter, Prince Jeord, but we have confirmed that there were no dangerous substances in the documentation..."

I accepted my capable servant's word and opened it, withdrawing a plain letter of sorts. What was written on the parchment, however, was... unimaginable.

"What... is this?"

I found myself at a loss for words.

★★★★★★★★★★

So apparently I had been kidnapped and brought to some unknown place, and on top of that, the kidnapper's goal wasn't a ransom? *I'm so confused! How am I supposed to handle a situation like this?*

However... when I was hungry, snacks would be brought to me. When I was bored and wished to read, they provided books, too. If I complained that my dresses were too stuffy or tight, I was brought some comfortable, relatively loose-fitting indoor clothing.

If I were at the academy, I'd be taking lessons and working hard at practical sessions. But now, while those events were happening, I was instead able to roll around and relax to my heart's content in this room.

If I were at Claes Manor, Mother would surely scold me while squinting those angled eyes of hers. *"How long do you intend to laze about, Katarina? You should be learning more about social etiquette and improving your manners!"* she'd say.

But here, no one would reproach me like that. I was free to enjoy all the books I could read, lie around in bed, and eat all the snacks I wanted. It had only been a little over half a day since I'd ended up in this strange place, but I had already found myself settling into a position of total comfort.

Lana seemed to find this strange. She stared at me with a doubtful expression. "Perhaps it would be strange, coming from someone in my position, Lady Katarina… but, if I may… are you not worried in the least?"

"Worried?"

"Well, yes… For instance, 'Where is this place?' 'Why was I taken?' All these remain unknowns…"

"Ah!" *Th-That's right! I've been… kidnapped!* I had been enjoying myself a little too much, to the point where I had forgotten all about this fact. "R-Right… kidnapped…" At Lana's words, I suddenly recalled my predicament and sputtered out a disjointed response.

"…Had you perhaps forgotten, Lady Katarina…?" Lana's blue eyes opened wide with shock. She seemed severely taken aback, or actually, more like completely dumbstruck.

"I… I apologize."

At my apology, Lana looked firmly downwards, not saying a word. Perhaps she was thinking about what a relaxed and silly fool of a girl I was. But like… really. I was in such a comfortable space, I really had no choice in the matter.

From the corner of my eye, I could see Lana's shoulders shivering violently. *Huh?! Wh-What's wrong? Is she ill?* "L-Lana? What's wrong? Are you okay?" I asked, worried.

"...N-No. No, it is nothing, Lady Katarina. Please do excuse me," she said, her voice somewhat unsteady.

"Are you... really alright?"

"Yes. Please do not worry," Lana replied, her voice now more normal than it had been. She then looked up, turning to face me. "You really are as the rumors say, Lady Katarina..." Her expression was now a beaming smile.

"Rumors?" I wondered what she meant by that.

But Lana simply laughed bewitchingly to herself, deflecting my question. That laughter... it was almost as if I had seen it somewhere before... But I was probably just overthinking things. After all, this was the first time I had met her.

Finally recalling my predicament, I attempted to obtain some information from Lana, but she was unable to answer, as expected. She was a maid, after all — if she'd been forbidden to speak about certain things by her masters, then it wouldn't be easy to get information from her. Then again... even if I told Anne to keep quiet about certain things, she never did. Like when I sneakily took snacks from the kitchen, or when I broke vases and statues while romping around, and all that. Those things were swiftly reported to Mother as soon as they happened.

And so, I continued living in that small room, relaxing and enjoying myself as much as I wanted. I also spoke a great deal with Lana, who stayed with me this whole time. I told her about the fields I'd tilled and the crops I'd planted, and the trees I'd climbed and fish I'd caught. She seemed entranced by my stories. She requested more tales with sparkling eyes, and we soon became steadfast friends.

This is bad... I could really, really get used to this new life of mine.

Lana brought me lunch, and I convinced her to stay and eat with me by complaining that eating alone was boring. Tonight's dinner, however, was completely different.

I was taken to a ridiculously long table where an elaborate spread of cutlery was laid out. I assumed that dinner would be served on this absurd table. A servant in the room indicated a spot that had been prepared for me, and I was soon seated there. There was another set of cutlery across from me, which made it seem like there would be another person joining me at the table.

Just as I became aware of this, Selena walked into the room, closely followed by that playboy butler. Upon seeing that I had sat myself obediently in my assigned chair, she called out to me. "Lady Katarina, are you feeling alright…?"

"Ah, yes. Sure! Thanks to your hospitality." It was a casual and even somewhat happy response — as if I had forgotten about my kidnapping all over again.

Selena seemed confused at my tone. "I sincerely apologize… I was unable to make the appropriate preparations for lunch, and I feel poorly for you, having lunch in that tiny room…" She bowed her head deeply.

It was worth noting that the nobles of this kingdom mostly had their meals in rooms like this dining room unless they were sick and bedridden. I supposed that was why Selena said what she did, but that room wasn't tiny to me by any means, and I didn't really need a huge variety of food. In fact, I had a tendency to attempt to eat everything that was presented to me, and I would get stomach aches due to this habit. But lunch today had been just the right amount of food, and I had eaten while having a lively discussion with Lana, so there was no need for Selena to apologize.

"Oh, no, please don't worry. I am absolutely fine!" I answered. I really was fine.

"…I sincerely apologize for these trying circumstances…" Selena, however, interpreted my declaration very differently. She bowed her head with a sorrowful expression, staring downward at her hands. Looking at her made me feel guilty!

On the surface, Selena looked like a sheltered, pampered noble lady… but she was surely a delicate and gentle person. At this point, I simply wanted to say, *"Oh, but I'm having quite a comfortable time!"* but surely this would be interpreted as yet another gesture of forced politeness.

Apparently Selena thinks I'm a delicate noble lady myself! But… no. Of course I'm nothing like that. Not delicate, for sure, though maybe a little sheltered. Though hey, I could be delicate at times if I tried. For example, I'd be upset if something I was planning to eat was taken by someone else first. Or when my crops, ripe for harvest, ended up eaten by birds and other pests, my delicate heart would suffer.

But that was not the case now. After all, I could eat everything I wanted, read whatever I felt like, roll around in bed all day and not have anyone yell at me… If this wasn't comfort, what was? In fact, I found myself wanting to live my elegant, fulfilling life in this place a little while longer.

Selena didn't understand my perspective at all. Instead, she only continued to apologize, constantly going out of her way to show her consideration. Even though I was eating eagerly, she said, "It's quite alright, Lady Katarina… you do not have to force yourself to eat it," all the while with a worried look. But of course, I was eating because I wanted to…

If anything, I now felt worried for Selena, who didn't seem very keen on eating anything at all. In fact, I started to wonder… Selena had been worried about me all this time, but what if she herself had been kidnapped too? She didn't look very healthy at all. Even so, she continued asking if there was anything I needed or wanted, time and time again. I already had more than enough of everything, really. I was given anything I could want.

Selena's consideration was really something else. In fact, I could say that her pampering of me had surpassed any other experience I'd had for the past sixteen years or so. Looking at Selena, I couldn't help but feel that this entire kidnapping affair couldn't possibly be something she'd intended to do. I had only spent a little bit of time with her, and yet I already knew that much.

With my meal finally over, I mentally patted myself on the back, feeling very full indeed. It was then that my gaze met with Lana's. Her eyes narrowed ever so slightly. *Th-This! This look is…! The look of exasperation at a foolish girl who's forgotten she's been kidnapped! But no! I haven't forgotten!* I had only slightly, slightly relaxed due to my newfound comfort. And so…

"Um… Lady Selena? May I know why I was brought here? You mentioned before that I would be released as soon as certain things were settled. What exactly are these… things?" I questioned Selena once again, with the very first question I had asked her in the beginning. *See? I haven't forgotten that I've been kidnapped at all! I was just happily enjoying some vacation time, and that's all there is to it!*

At my question, Selena, who had only looked mildly ill before, now seemed very, very sick indeed. *Ugh… I apologize, Selena. Really, I do.*

"Yes… I suppose you would be most uncomfortable being left in the dark, Lady Katarina… Maybe this will even affect your quality of sleep…"

Well, no… I had been treated very well. I wasn't fearful or worried at all, and I was very confident that I would be able to fall asleep soundly at night. Even so, I held my peace and allowed Selena to speak.

"In truth, Lady Katarina… you have been brought here because…"

As soon as Selena had started to speak, that playboy butler of hers, Rufus, quickly interrupted her. "Lady Selena… you have already finished your meal. Perhaps you should return to your chambers? You must be tired too, Lady Katarina… it would be best for you to get some sleep," Rufus said, placing a single hand on Selena's shoulder.

"…I see… yes. Well then, Lady Katarina… goodnight." With that, Selena rose from her seat, looking like an emotionless doll, before turning and leaving the room altogether.

It was as if she had become a different person than the Selena I had been speaking to earlier. For some reason, I felt a slight tingle… an unpleasant shiver down my spine.

In the end, I didn't find out where or why I was being held captive — and soon, it was nighttime. Although Selena was worried about me being unable to sleep, I didn't have any problem at all. After dinner I chatted happily with Lana, had some delicious tea while I was at it, and soon was off to the land of slumber. In fact, I had already elegantly slipped into a deep sleep, when…

"Lady Katarina, please wake up."

"No… I don't want… to. Sleepy. Let me sleep a bit more, Anne."

127

"I regret to inform you, Lady Katarina, that I am not Anne, but Lana."

"Nn… Lana?" *Huh? It isn't Anne? Who's Lana again?*

Finally opening my eyes, I was greeted with an unfamiliar ceiling — this wasn't the dormitory room I was used to. *Hm? Where am I again?* With my memories muddled, I sat up slowly, finally remembering the events of the day before. That's right… I'd been kidnapped and brought to this comfortable room.

The room was dark, only illuminated dimly by the faint glow of the bedside lamp. *Huh…? It still isn't quite morning yet.*

"You have a guest, Lady Katarina."

"Hm…? Guest?" *Who could it be, at this time of the night?* I sleepily got up from bed, had Lana do my hair and straighten my nightgown — all while I was half asleep — before finally sitting down in a chair. With that, the door quietly opened, and standing in the frame was a small, familiar silhouette.

"…Selena?" The person illuminated by my lamp was Selena Berg. She was so cute that I couldn't help but see her as some sort of small animal. *But… what is it, at this time? Ugh… really… I'm still so sleepy.* I rubbed my eyes groggily.

"Yes… I do apologize for visiting you at this hour, Lady Katarina… However, I could not help but be worried that you would be filled with fear, and hence unable to sleep…"

Actually, it was Selena who seemed like she hadn't slept. She looked visibly more haggard than she had earlier. I, on the other hand, had been treated to a delicious dinner and had fallen asleep comfortably soon after. I would assume this showed on my face, so any onlooker would instantly be more concerned about Selena instead.

"…At the dinner table just now… for some reason, I felt this strong feeling that I should not tell you something. But… I still feel that it is important to tell you," Selena said, something obviously weighing on her mind. To think that she had been worried for me all this time as I comfortably laid down and fell asleep… Now I felt sorry too.

"Hmm… The reason I was brought to this place, right? So you *do* know the reason."

"Yes… after all, this entire kidnapping was planned by me…"

"Wha?!" *Lady Selena is the culprit? With her acting so guilty, I'd thought that she was being used by someone, or maybe even being threatened… but it turns out that she was the mastermind…!* My jaw hung loosely as I gaped like a goldfish in suspended surprise.

As if repenting, Selena began her exposition. "I… I wanted to kidnap you, Lady Katarina… and use your safety as a bargaining chip. All so that Prince Jeord would abandon his claim to the throne…"

"…Jeord? To make him give up on the throne?" I supposed that would make sense.

"Yes… So that Prince Ian may take the throne instead." Up until now, Selena's eyes had been dark, even slightly clouded, but now I saw the clear shine of resolve in them.

And then she continued, and the secrets behind this kidnapping began to unravel…

There were a lot of complicated bits here and there, but I understood most of it. To summarize, Jeord had been gaining in political strength recently, and a certain faction of nobles felt that the throne should go to him.

Before this, the struggle was between Jeffrey, oldest of the four princes, and Ian, the second oldest prince. Competition would only increase in intensity if Jeord threw his hat into the ring too. This was why she wanted Jeord to give up on his claim to the throne before that could happen.

Why then, wasn't this done to Ian's biggest rival, Jeffrey? Why Jeord? I did wonder about that, but in any case…

"Well… even in exchange for my safety, I doubt that Prince Jeord would simply give up his claim to the throne." While it was true that I had been friends with Jeord for almost nine years, and we got along well, throwing aside the claim to a royal throne wasn't something to be taken lightly.

Would Jeord even do such a thing? If I were his lover or wife, maybe that would make sense, but I was nothing more than his fiancée, only there to deter others. I didn't think that Jeord would go that far for someone like me.

"You jest, Lady Katarina… Prince Jeord's love for you is well known throughout the land. He would do anything — anything at all for you, Lady Katarina…" Selena said passionately.

Alas… that's nothing more than a false rumor! All for the sake of preventing annoying noble ladies from approaching that black-hearted, sadist prince. Or so I thought.

"I am… most envious, Lady Katarina… so envious… that he loves you so, so much…" Selena said, her cheeks softly illuminated by the lamplight. I felt like I shouldn't crush her dreams, so I kept silent about it.

★★★★★★★★★

Prince Jeord, Prince Alan, Master Keith, Master Nicol, Lady Mary, Lady Sophia, and Lady Maria… along with other members of the student council, were all gathered in a certain room in this dormitory. However, one figure who should have been in this room was missing. I, Anne Shelly, was missing my mistress, Lady Katarina Claes.

About half a day had passed since the end of the school festival… since the young miss had disappeared. It was then that an anonymous letter had arrived at Prince Jeord's doorstep. Written within were these simple words: *"If you wish for the safe return of Katarina Claes, publicly renounce your claim to the throne at once."*

Lady Katarina was still missing, her whereabouts unknown. She had been kidnapped.

Upon receiving the letter, Prince Jeord had called for everyone and explained the situation. Having noticed my ever-growing worry for the young miss, he was considerate enough to allow me to stay for this meeting.

As soon as Prince Jeord had finished his explanation, the expressions of all who were present, which were already clouded before, now became even more ominous. I suspected that my expression, too, was one of horror and shock.

A heavy silence filled the room as the explanation ended. Not a single word was spoken for quite some time… and then.

"Well? What do you intend to do, Prince Jeord?" Master Keith said, staring pointedly at the prince.

"If this is all I have to do to bring Katarina back safely, I'll renounce it. Crown, throne, and all. However… I cannot do this immediately. It is a process, and time is required. If, during this time, anything happens…" Prince Jeord's usual smile was nowhere to be seen. His expression was grave — and almost as severe as Master Nicol's.

131

"...Even should you comply, we have no guarantees of Katarina's safety. Consider the fact that she may be... silenced by the perpetrator, for having seen their face." Master Nicol's words were heavy.

"No! No! That cannot be! To take her suddenly and kill her just because she saw who they were, it would be so senseless!" Lady Sophia cried, although her voice was more like a wail of sorrow. Although I did not have the words, I screamed silently in my heart along with her.

"It's someone capable of kidnapping, yeah? There's no sense with these types. It's very possible, what Nicol's saying. We don't have any guarantee that this will all end just because Jeord does what they want. Rather than starting some long-winded preparation to renounce the throne... we should be searching for where these people are."

"Oh, you do have good ideas sometimes, Prince Alan."

"...The 'sometimes' is unnecessary, Mary."

"Heheh. Do excuse me. So... in this case, all we have to do is utterly crush and destroy the place these unsavory types are hiding at, yes?" Lady Mary said, a somewhat ominous smile crossing her features.

Master Keith, however, raised a protest. "Well, no... searching haphazardly for these places would not be efficient. To begin with, it would take too much time..."

"U-Um...! Wasn't there a possibility of Dark Magic being involved in this incident in some way...?" Lady Maria said, her voice raising in desperation.

Yes… It would appear that all the students who should have seen Lady Katarina before her disappearance at the festival had all reported inexplicable gaps in their memory. This was very similar to the incident that occurred last year. Dark Magic was a forbidden power that was hidden from the masses by the royal family. The Dark Arts could control and manipulate the hearts of man…

The only reason why those gathered here knew of it at all was because of what had happened last year. During that time, a spell was cast on Lady Katarina, and she fell into a deep, unwaking slumber for some time. Everyone involved was intensely worried, but everything was eventually resolved peacefully, in no small part due to Lady Katarina's contributions.

Over the course of that incident, the secret of Dark Magic was revealed to everyone here, Lady Katarina, and me, on the account that I had been serving Lady Katarina all these years.

Yet, the Dark Magic incident of the previous year had been resolved. The culprit, too, now got along well with everyone in this room. As such, given that the Dark Arts were involved in this incident once more, we had no choice to think that another Wielder of Darkness was responsible.

"If… Dark Magic was used, I may be able to detect it, should I see any suspicious individuals," Lady Maria said. Being one of the few Wielders of Light in the kingdom, she was able to see what most could not — she was apparently capable of perceiving Dark Magic itself. As she said, perhaps she would be able to find the culprit, as long as she got a good look at them. It was a most effective idea, or so I thought.

"A fair idea, yes… However, as I recall, Dark Magic can only be perceived while it is being used, or a short while after, no? In that case… given that half a day has already passed, wouldn't it be no longer possible to discern…?"

"…That…" Lady Maria's expression clouded over.

Ahh… I thought that it was such a good idea, too…

"I suppose we simply have to crush the possibilities one by one, then!"

"Wait, Mary! Where do you think you're going? Calm down!"

Ignoring Prince Alan's protests, Lady Mary simply slipped by him, and with the most dark and ominous smile I had ever seen, placed her hand on the doorknob… just as a resounding series of knocks came from the other side. Another guest.

"Lady Mary… just where are you going?"

"Oh, if it isn't Master Raphael. It's good to see you. Of course, I'm heading out to begin my search for Lady Katarina."

This young man, Master Raphael Wolt, was the very same person who had caused the incident last year. He now worked for the Magical Ministry. He must have heard of the circumstances as well.

Master Raphael calmly responded to Lady Mary's words without a single shred of surprise. "And how do you intend to go about doing that, Lady Mary?"

"Well, I suppose we should start by utterly destroying whatever location seems suspicious. I intend to do just that."

Master Raphael merely sighed at Lady Mary, who seemed very confident in what she had just declared. "Would that not be a touch too reckless?"

"But while we all stand around talking, Lady Katarina is in the maws of danger! What do you suggest we all do, then?!" Lady Mary shouted. I could see tears brimming in her eyes. Despite her brave front, it was clear to us all that she, too, was deeply worried.

Master Raphael, however, smiled gently in response. "It is quite alright. Lady Katarina is in no danger whatsoever."

135

At this statement, Prince Jeord's eyes narrowed, his gaze directed squarely at Master Raphael. "Perhaps you should elaborate on your statement."

"Ah, but of course. You see, a fearsomely strong bodyguard of sorts is currently by Lady Katarina's side... and so, there is no immediate danger to her being. Please, let us wait just a little while longer." Following this statement, Master Raphael's tone of voice changed — it was now determined and forceful as he declared: "I will save Lady Katarina."

★★★★★★★★★★

It had now been a while since I'd started rubbing the sobbing Selena's back. I had no idea what to do anymore.

This had all started with talk of Jeord being willing to do anything for me — a misunderstanding, of course. Then Selena, with her cheeks illuminated by the lamplight, said, "I am most envious, Lady Katarina... that he loves you so, so much..." She repeated herself immediately after, sounding sorrowful. "I really, really am envious of you..." Soon, streams of tears were flowing from her large eyes.

"S-Selena! Are you alright? What's wrong?" Panicking, I approached her and placed a hand on her back.

"...Lady Katarina... to think that you would be worried about someone like me, someone who has done something like this to you... You really are a saint, just as the rumors say. Compared to you, I... I am really no good. Of course Prince Ian would hate me for who I am..." With that, Selena's sobbing intensified.

Rumors? Saint? I didn't understand what she was talking about, but now she was crying — no, sobbing. I couldn't think of anything to do but hold her close and rub her back as gently as I could. I continued this mildly soothing back-rubbing for a while until Selena finally calmed down enough to speak.

"I… I apologize. I lost my composure…" Her eyes were bloodshot, and she looked like she could collapse at any moment. "…I was just a little envious of Prince Jeord and you…"

"Envious?" *I'm just a suitor-deterrent for a sadistic, black-hearted prince! My position isn't enviable at all! It seems that she thinks Jeord and I are lovers of some kind…*

"Yes… The way you and Prince Jeord love and support each other is truly wonderful."

Hmm. Yep, a complete misunderstanding.

"It is not just you, but also Prince Jeffrey and Lady Susanna, and Prince Alan and Lady Mary… They all support each other as equals, and I am envious of that."

I don't know much about Prince Jeffrey and his partner, but… are Mary and Alan equals in their relationship? If anything, it feels like Mary always has the upper hand. In fact, the sight of Alan escorting Mary often looked like an enforcer escorting their mob boss.

But that wasn't something I could just blurt out to Selena at a time like this. So I held my peace and listened to what she had to say.

"Lady Susanna is known as one of the wisest and most talented women in the kingdom…"

Ohh? So that sexy lady is known like that, huh?

"Lady Mary is known as the epitome of an ideal noble lady…"

Ah, yes. Mary is really something else. She's great at dance and social etiquette… She's perfect in every way. In fact, that's why she has Alan as her subordinate!

"Lady Katarina is known as a saint, accepting and gracious…"

Huh?! Me? A saint? People say that about me?! Sorry to disappoint, but I've never heard of such a thing! No one has ever referred to me like that.

Did they really mean "a saint"? Maybe they meant to say that I had a lot of sass. Surely it must be a mistake like that. After all, my instructors always used to tell me that I'm "full of sass and spirit." High praise indeed!

"Compared to everyone else... I am good at nothing. Good for nothing. My magic is weak... and I am not very smart. I could never hope to support Prince Ian... I am nothing more than baggage for him, a failure of a fiancée..." Selena said, tears returning to her eyes. "So... at the very least, I wanted to be of some use to him... and so I plotted this entire incident. I truly apologize, Lady Katarina..." The tears started flowing all over again.

Weak magic... and not too smart? I couldn't help but feel a sense of camaraderie with Selena. I now understood why she was feeling so guilty all this time, and I could see the reason behind all this happening.

Although her methods were somewhat questionable, all Selena wanted to do was be useful to someone she loved. When I thought about it that way, I couldn't help but feel warmly towards her.

"Of course... I plan to take responsibility for all this, once it is over."

"Huh? Responsibility?"

"Yes... I will call off my engagement with Prince Ian, and as a means of atoning for my sins, I will turn myself in to the authorities..." Selena declared, without a shred of hesitation in her eyes.

Wha?! Call off her engagement and turn herself in? But why?

"Wh-Why? You're just trying to do something for Prince Ian, right? But now you're planning on calling off your engagement with him and turning yourself in? Is that really what you want?"

"Yes… I was the one who started admiring Prince Ian in the first place. And now I have made up my mind. I am resolved."

"Huh? But aren't you two engaged?" The way Selena spoke, it was like her love towards Prince Ian was one-sided.

Selena, however, merely continued on sadly. "I was born to a duke. When I was young, I spent time with Prince Ian, and due to my age and the fact that I could use magic, I was selected as his fiancée. But as I said before, my magical capability is low… and I am not good at my studies. Before long, both my parents and my relatives started suggesting that he should look for a more fitting fiancée. Of course they would think that. The partners of the other princes are all remarkable! They all support each other in some way. I alone am no good. I alone am lacking… I only hold Prince Ian back."

Well… back at Claes Manor, my mother was always saying, *"Prince Jeord should select another fiancée! My daughter will do nothing but hold him back!"* and stuff like that. *Hmm, yes.* I now felt closer to Selena than ever. We were so alike in many ways.

Selena continued on, all the while having no idea of the thoughts going through my mind. "Also… Prince Ian himself has nothing but contempt for me, so…" She bowed her head dejectedly.

Prince Ian hates Selena? Really? I thought about that day at the school festival. Prince Ian, strict and rigid, with the most serious expression, escorting Selena. There was no way I could possibly know much about their relationship from that encounter alone, so…

"Well… Have you ever heard Prince Ian himself say that to you…?"

"Huh?"

"Have you ever asked Prince Ian how he truly feels about you?"

"Th-There is no way I could ask him something like that! But then… everyone around me always talks about how Prince Ian is tired of me, how he dislikes me… and how he… already hates me…"

"But Lady Selena… those are the words of other people, right? Have you heard the prince himself say it? Maybe you're just imagining that he hates you?"

"But…"

You shouldn't ever pay too much attention to what others say. This was especially true for noble society, according to my wise brother, Keith. *"Insults and slander are common occurrences in noble society, Big Sister. Pay them no heed,"* he would say.

If one were to believe those slanders and lies, one may actually believe that I was some splendid and amazing noble lady, well-loved by Prince Jeord, when the opposite was true. And so…

"Someone's emotions can only be known by that person themselves, right? So, Lady Selena… if you wish to know the truth, you have to ask Prince Ian, and that's that!"

"Ask…?" Selena raised her bowed head.

"Yes, speak to Prince Ian about it, or at least try!" After all, nothing would happen without an actual conversation about it. In fact, this was the case with Selena herself — it was only through talking to her now that I developed a deeper understanding of her.

Selena opened her large, round eyes wide, her brown irises staring straight at me.

"Say… Lady Selena. You've been saying that you were no good, that you are lacking, just now… and I don't think that's true."

Honestly speaking, given the lack of magical aptitude and academic ability that Selena was concerned about, we weren't very different. After all, we just happened to be in an academy where there was a disproportionately high number of high-spec people.

"More importantly, you were worried about me, a complete stranger. You were worried if I could sleep. And you even have the resolve to get captured and sentenced... all in the name of helping someone you love."

That kind of bravery would be impossible for me. And on top of that, she mustered up this resolve all while under the assumption that the person she loved disliked her! Compared to me, who had come up with a variety of contingency plans like realistic snake toys in case Jeord ever attacked me, the difference was stark.

I returned Selena's gaze, looking deep into her brown eyes. "To me, Lady Selena, you are gentle and strong. There's not a single bone in you that is lacking or no-good. I think you are a wonderful person."

Selena's eyes widened in surprise — and for a while, she only stared at me. "...That's the... first time... anyone has said anything like that to me..."

I smiled slightly at the stunned Selena. "Well then! I'll keep saying it from here on out. As many times as you'd like. So... would you like to be friends, Lady Selena?"

Although she was the one who looked worse for wear, all Selena did was worry about me. She was willing to get captured and sentenced, all for the sake of someone she loved. Although she was small in stature and had mannerisms like a small animal, Lady Selena was strong. She was a pure-hearted, strong noble lady.

It was a strange, maybe alarming relationship, given that she was the kidnapper and I was the victim, but... in this short span of time, I had come to like Selena Berg. More than anything else, my sense of camaraderie with her had increased throughout our conversation. We would definitely get along well.

I smiled, extending a hand towards Selena.

"…To say such words towards one who kidnapped you… Lady Katarina, you truly are as the rumors say," Selena said as she stared at my outstretched hand.

Hmm? Rumors? Ah, was this about the sassy and spirited thing?

"…Even though I have done such a thing… I would like to be friends…"

And with that, Lady Selena took my hand. She returned my gaze now, no longer averting her eyes.

"Lady Katarina… As you said, I won't be swayed by what others say anymore. I will speak with Prince Ian himself and hear what he has to say."

"Yes, that's a good start!"

"…Yes." Selena's eyes were no longer filled with tears, and her troubled, sickly expression had lifted. "But before that… I really need to stop this foolish kidnapping affair… and also atone for my sins…"

"If it ever comes down to it, I'll keep it a secret!" After all, Selena hadn't done anything terrible to me. If anything, she had provided me with quite a comfortable life! It was like someone going out for a walk and getting a little lost.

Selena smiled somewhat bitterly at my words. "You really are a gentle person, through and through… however… that is simply not acceptable. Sins committed by my hand have to be atoned for appropriately…" she said with a calm and dignified expression.

Ah, this girl really is a pure and strong person, despite her cute appearance… The more I looked at her, the more I felt like I would fall for her.

"Well then… I shall see to it that you are safely delivered back to Prince Jeord this instant. I shall begin making the preparations…" Saying so, Selena stood up and headed towards the door.

The moment she placed her hand on the handle, however, she collapsed — no, her body had gone completely limp.

"L-Lady Selena!" Alarmed, I rushed to her side, only to notice then that someone had stepped through the door to the room.

"I had only taken my eye off you momentarily, and here you are, doing as you please. This is most troubling… Lady Selena," the man said, placing a hand on the fallen Selena as he did so. A ravishing smile lit up his face.

"Y-You! What have you done to Lady Selena?"

What he'd just said and his tone of voice… It was obvious that this man had done something to her. I glared daggers at him.

"Just letting her sleep for a while. After all, she still does have her role to play."

"R-Role?"

"Yes, of course. That of a scapegoat — this kidnapping, and a multitude of other sins will all be pinned on her. Then… I shall have her disappear with Prince Ian. That is her role."

"Ah!"

"And you shall disappear as well, Lady Katarina Claes… with Prince Jeord by your side."

The man who spoke was Rufus, Selena's playboy butler. He was smiling with enjoyment and anticipation.

★★★★★★★★★★

The first time I, Selena Berg, met him... I was nine years of age.

The boy who I met then was a beautiful person. Beauty the likes of which I had never seen before... All I could do was freeze up, overcome with nervousness.

"I-It is good to m-meet you... I-I... My name is Selena B-Berg... it is a p-pleasure to make your acquaintance..." Although I had practiced my greetings so much, that was what I was reduced to in my nervousness.

The adults around me started to laugh under their breaths. I could feel my face heating up from the embarrassment... surely, my face was all red. The very thought of that deepened my humiliation, and I simply looked down at my feet. But then—

"It is nice to meet you as well, Selena. My name is Ian Stuart. The pleasure is all mine," he said with an expression of utmost seriousness, stretching out his hand.

Although the people around me laughed at my fumbled greetings and reddened face, he did not laugh at me. He extended his warm hand towards me. It was then that the young me fell for him — just like that.

That was my first meeting with Prince Ian. I was born into the family of a duke, was the same age as the prince, and had already started manifesting my magical abilities. That was the reason why I had been chosen as the fiancée of Ian Stuart, the second prince of the kingdom.

The emotions of the individuals involved hardly came into play in such a marriage. But... I met Prince Ian, and I fell in love with him. Ever since then, my budding feelings for him continued to grow. The way he was so serious and focused... the way he was gentle and caring, but not very good at showing it... the more I spent time with him, the more my feelings blossomed.

Before I knew it, ten years had passed since I had been assigned as his fiancée. Now, more than anything, I loved Prince Ian. I loved him very much. Although my love for him grew and grew... I was lacking. My magical aptitude was the reason why I had been chosen as his fiancée in the first place, but my magical capabilities never increased.

I worked hard to be able to stand by Prince Ian's side. No matter how hard I tried, however, my magic remained weak. Perhaps then I could simply do well in my studies, I thought... but I did not manage to do too well academically either.

Although I was born with magic and was attending the same academy as Prince Ian and many others, I was not chosen as a student council member. The council was admired by the student body, and such a role was considered an honor. Prince Jeffrey, Lady Susanna, and Prince Ian were all selected, too. I was the odd one out. I alone was the underdog.

In addition, Prince Jeffrey was always found with Lady Susanna as a pair. They were really close... and yet, this was not the case with Prince Ian and myself. Unless there was something he wanted, he would never meet with me. He would never touch me when we saw each other, either, unless it was absolutely necessary. He was always focused on pursuing his goals and needs single-mindedly.

This did not go unnoticed by those around us. Soon, the rumors started flowing. *"Prince Ian dislikes his incapable fiancée,"* they would say.

Prince Ian and I graduated from the Academy of Magic. Next to enroll in the academy were his younger twin brothers, Prince Jeord and Prince Alan, along with their respective fiancées. I had heard that both of the Princes had been chosen as student council members, as was Lady Mary, Prince Alan's fiancée.

145

Although Prince Jeord's fiancée, Lady Katarina, was not chosen for the council, she was well-admired by the student body, and even had her own fan group. When word of this got out to noble circles, my parents and relatives all started saying the same thing. *"Perhaps the Prince should look for a more fitting fiancée..."* they would say.

Amidst the dazzling individuals that were these princes and their fiancées, I couldn't help but feel that I alone was incompatible... that I could not measure up to them. Why was I so inept? Given that I could never be better than the average person no matter how hard I tried... of course it would be a given that Prince Ian would come to dislike me.

Even so, I still wanted to be of use to him. Anything was fine. Something... anything. If it meant that I could do something for him to make up for all the trouble I had caused up until now...

As those thoughts filled my mind and my heart, that person appeared before me.

"Allow me to assist you with your wish."

With that, he began telling me exactly how I could be of use to Prince Ian...

When I entered her room, she had already awoken, and was staring in my direction with her aqua-blue eyes.

"I see you have awoken safely... Most reassuring," I said, feeling relieved from the bottom of my heart.

When I had brought her into the manor, she was barely conscious. Although we had only used a small amount of the sleep-inducing drug on her, I remained worried. I simply had to see with my own eyes that she was alright.

After affirming her safety, there was something I absolutely had to tell her now that she was awake. I apologized to her and assured her that she would be allowed to go once things were settled. Then I bowed deeply to the fiancée of Prince Jeord, Lady Katarina Claes.

Even if it was all for Prince Ian's sake, me bringing an unrelated noble lady to this place was an unforgivable transgression. I understood that. That was why I thought I should apologize first — precisely because I had done an unforgivable thing to Lady Katarina.

Upon hearing my words, Lady Katarina was momentarily silent, as if deep in thought. And then, her lips parted. "...Kidnapped...?"

I was terribly surprised. How could this be? Nothing had been explained to her, and yet, she had already realized that she had been kidnapped. According to the rumors, Lady Katarina was spirited and strong, but yet one who possessed a deep well of compassion. In reality, it would seem like she was a very intelligent person as well.

I apologized deeply once again, though I knew that I would not be forgiven either way. Lady Katarina began to think once more, a serious expression clouding her features. "...Um. Well then... how much would the ransom be...?" she said.

"Ran...som?" I did not understand the meaning of this word, and simply repeated it back at her. Lady Katarina leaned in slightly with a somewhat grave expression.

"Yes. The amount of gold you want in exchange for my safety. How much would it be...?"

"...Ah, no. We do not have any intention of asking for a... sum of gold." Lady Katarina had apparently assumed that we had kidnapped her for money. I denied it as quickly as I could.

"Huh? It's not gold you're after? Then why did you kidnap me?"

Of course, she did not know why she'd been taken. Surely she was unsettled by this, and would be unable to feel at ease until she knew the answer.

"...That is..." *I got her involved in all this. I should tell Lady Katarina about the entire affair.* I started to speak, wanting to explain the situation, but then...

"Lady Selena. You have already ascertained Lady Katarina's safety, have you not? Please, let us return to your quarters." Rufus placed a hand on my shoulder.

Ahh... yes. That's right... I felt like I simply had to return to my room. "Rufus... yes. Yes, let's. Well then, Lady Katarina... I shall return to my quarters..."

"Wha...? P-Please wait..."

"I do apologize... Lana, please take care of her. Lady Katarina... if you are wanting for anything, anything at all... please inform Lana of your needs. We will aim to provide for you as best as we can."

With that, I returned to my room, with Rufus guiding me... But there was still a lingering sense of unease in my heart.

After returning from my visit to Lady Katarina's quarters, I felt... blank, for some reason. I could feel some vague gaps in my memory.

I stayed in a haze for quite some time. Before I knew it, lunch had already passed, and I was unable to present the meal to Lady Katarina properly. When I found out that she had her meal in the room she was confined in, I felt incredibly guilty. She had been suddenly brought to this strange place without knowing why, and then was confined in that small room... She would surely be worried and uneasy.

She was spirited and strong like the rumors had said, but she could very well be putting on a brave front for me. For all I knew, she could be crying this very moment. When I thought about that, even though I was the one who had decided to do all of this to begin with — my chest began to hurt.

At the very least, I wanted Lady Katarina to feel comfortable, even if it would only be a small consolation. I decided that only the finest ingredients should be used when preparing dinner.

After the preparations were complete, Rufus and I made for the hall where dinner had been prepared, and found Lady Katarina already sitting on a chair

"Lady Katarina, are you feeling alright…?"

"Ah, yes. Sure! Thanks to your hospitality."

"I sincerely apologize… I was unable to make the appropriate preparations for lunch, and I feel poorly for you, having lunch in that tiny room…" I bowed once more, apologizing for the way Lady Katarina had to take her lunch.

"Oh, no, please don't worry. I am absolutely fine!" she answered without wavering in the slightest.

But she had been locked in this room and informed that she had been kidnapped! There was no way Lady Katarina could possibly be fine… Surely she was pushing herself to put up a brave front for my sake. I could feel the pain in my chest intensifying.

I apologized yet again. That was all I was capable of doing. How pathetic of me…

As we began having our dinner, Lady Katarina showed no signs of distress. She continued pretending that she was completely fine. I grew even more worried about her.

"It's quite alright, Lady Katarina… you do not have to force yourself to eat it," I said, only for her to respond to me with a gentle smile.

Then she unexpectedly asked after me, noticing that I did not have very much to eat. "Are you okay, Lady Selena?" she asked.

149

She asked me that, even though she was clearly the one who was in a more painful, distressing situation. Lady Katarina really was a saint.

After the final courses of dinner had been served, Lady Katarina questioned me once again. "Um… Lady Selena? May I know why I was brought here? You mentioned before that I would be released as soon as certain things were settled. What exactly are these… things?"

But of course, there was no way Lady Katarina wouldn't be bothered by this. She must have been uncertain and worried all this time. And yet, she tried so hard to appear calm and collected. It hurt. The pain in my chest intensified yet again. I felt so, so remorseful. Perhaps it was best to tell her now…

"In truth, Lady Katarina… you have been brought here because…"

But then, Rufus interrupted me the moment I started to speak. "Lady Selena… you have already finished your meal. Perhaps you should return to your chambers? You must be tired too, Lady Katarina… it would be best for you to get some sleep."

He placed a hand on my shoulder. With that, suddenly, the notion that it would be better not to tell Lady Katarina anything filled my mind.

…*Perhaps it is best if I speak nothing of it.* I had to return to my room, just like Rufus said. I had to listen to him — I simply had to. After all… Rufus was a really kind person. He was the one who told me how I could be useful to Prince Ian.

"…I see… yes. Well then, Lady Katarina… goodnight."

I had to return to my room and rest… but why? My heart felt uneasy once again.

Upon returning to my room, I sat down on a chair, and for a while, thought of… nothing. Was it just me, or… were these incidents occurring more as of late? Before I knew it, night had already fallen. My room was enveloped in darkness.

Just when I thought I should move over to my bed and lie down, an image flashed through my mind.

"Are you okay, Lady Selena?"

…Those aqua-blue eyes… Lady Katarina!

Why did all my thoughts about Lady Katarina evaporate when I returned to my room? I had done terrible things to her. Kidnap her, lock her up in that room, and yet, this saint-like girl was still kind to me.

How could I have forgotten about something like that…? I really was no good at all… Utterly contemptible. Would Lady Katarina be tossing and turning right about now, unable to fall asleep?

I had to go… I had to go to her, and do for her what little I could. That was the very least I could do.

In the quiet of night, I crept out of my room as the entire manor slumbered. As I placed one foot in front of another in the darkened halls of the manor, I could feel my head clearing up… for reasons unknown to me.

When I finally reached Lady Katarina's room, I was greeted by a maid standing by her door. She was a recent hire, taken on in preparation for this kidnapping plan. Now, she was a maid assigned to Lady Katarina — Lana. She had a look of utter seriousness about her, as if she had been standing in front of that door, guarding it this whole time. I asked Lana if that was the case, only for her to answer, "I just awoke a short while ago."

I informed Lana that I would like to meet with Lady Katarina. "One moment, my lady," she said, before entering the room. After a short period of time, I heard Lana's muffled voice call out from within, "Please enter."

"...Selena?" Lady Katarina seemed confused — slightly disoriented, perhaps.

"Yes... I do apologize for visiting you at this hour, Lady Katarina... However, I could not help but be worried that you would be filled with fear, and hence unable to sleep..."

Lady Katarina rubbed her eyes as I approached her. Surely she had been weeping moments before... *What have I done?* I made up my mind. I had to speak to Lady Katarina — do what I could to alleviate a small part of her unease.

"...At the dinner table just now... for some reason, I felt this strong feeling that I should not tell you something. But... I still feel that it is important to tell you."

"Hmm... The reason I was brought to this place, right? So you *do* know the reason."

"Yes... after all, this entire kidnapping was planned by me..."

"Wha?!" Lady Katarina seemed terribly surprised.

I started telling her everything — the truth behind this entire incident, about how I had kidnapped her in order to force Prince Jeord to cast away his claim to the throne. All so that Prince Ian may take the throne instead.

It had all started several months ago. The young man known as Rufus Brode, hailing from a family distantly related to ours, was introduced to us. He performed well in all his tasks, and served me diligently despite the fact that I was largely ignored by my family because of how useless I was.

Rufus never once complained about my failings. He would always be supportive and helpful, and had nothing but kind words for me. It was to him, and no other, that I eventually told my thoughts to.

Whatever happens, it would be fine… so long as I can be useful to Prince Ian. This thought that I held strongly in my mind.

Upon hearing this, Rufus said, *"Allow me to assist you with your wish."* And then, he thought of a plan to force all the rival princes to forsake their claims to the throne so that Prince Ian would be king.

When I had first heard about the plan, I was terrified. I felt that it was all but impossible for me to do such things. But then, Rufus reminded me… *"It is for Prince Ian. This is the only thing you could possibly do for him."* The more I listened to his passionate words, the more convinced I became.

After that, Rufus suggested a plan — a scheme to entrap and kidnap Lady Katarina. That was the first step we would take.

I told Lady Katarina about everything — with the exception of Rufus' involvement. Why did I leave his name out of the explanation…? Because he had done so, so much for me. If I brought him up, he would be implicated in many crimes too, and I felt horrible thinking of it.

After hearing my explanation, Lady Katarina was silent for a while, as if deep in thought. And then she said, "Well… even in exchange for my safety, I doubt that Prince Jeord would simply give up his claim to the throne."

Her words surprised me. I felt compelled to offer a swift response. "You jest, Lady Katarina… Prince Jeord's love for you is well known throughout the land. He would do anything — anything at all for you, Lady Katarina…"

After all, Prince Jeord's love for Lady Katarina, and how he spoiled her, was a known fact in the noble circles of society. Honestly, Prince Jeord's expression when he was escorting Lady Katarina at his birthday party was one of true happiness.

"I am… most envious, Lady Katarina… so envious… that he loves you so, so much…"

Loved by Prince Jeord, praised and admired by so many around her… Compared to her, I was…

"I really, really am envious of you…" The words were escaping my lips before I even knew it. I was no-good. Useless. I could not support my prince — unlike the other princes' fiancées. The more I thought about that, the more a suffocating sadness enveloped me. I was pathetic. Pitiful. Soon, tears were flowing down my cheeks.

"S-Selena! Are you alright? What's wrong?" With those words, Lady Katarina approached me, placing an arm around me and her hand on my back.

"…Lady Katarina… to think that you would be worried about someone like me, someone who has done something like this to you… You really are a saint, just as the rumors say. Compared to you, I… I am really no good. Of course Prince Ian would hate me for who I am…"

Lady Katarina was called a saint at the academy. She was not tied to any notions of status, treated everyone equally, and was a person overflowing with passion. The fiancée of a prince, and from a noble family. I had thought that the rumors were exaggerated, perhaps… yet although she was the victim of this entire kidnapping, she was showing kindness to me — the perpetrator. Surely it was Lady Katarina herself who wished to shed tears, and yet here she was, gently rubbing my back, all the while without showing a single sign of anger.

Lady Katarina was such a wonderful person, truly befitting of the title of saint. It was a given that such an amazing person would be dearly loved by Prince Jeord.

The gentle motions of her hand on my back slowly allowed me to calm down. I apologized for losing my composure, and told her that I was envious.

"Envious?"

"Yes... The way you and Prince Jeord love and support each other is truly wonderful. It is not just you, but also Prince Jeffrey and Lady Susanna, and Prince Alan and Lady Mary... They all support each other as equals, and I am envious of that."

Lady Katarina continued to comfort me. It was as if a dam had broken inside me — large droplets of tears fell as I felt the gentle touch of her hand.

"Lady Susanna is known as one of the wisest and most talented women in the kingdom... Lady Mary is known as the epitome of an ideal noble lady... Lady Katarina is known as a saint, accepting and gracious..."

All of them were talented and admirable. They were all worthy of being fiancées to princes.

"Compared to everyone else... I am good at nothing. Good for nothing. My magic is weak... and I am not very smart. I could never hope to support Prince Ian... I am nothing more than baggage for him, a failure of a fiancée... So... at the very least, I wanted to be of some use to him... and so I plotted this entire incident. I truly apologize, Lady Katarina..."

All I could do now was apologize. But I then explained that I intended to take responsibility once this was over.

"Huh? Responsibility?"

"Yes… I will call off my engagement with Prince Ian, and as a means of atoning for my sins, I will turn myself in to the authorities…"

This had been determined the moment we decided to go ahead with this kidnapping plan. Relinquishing one's claim to the throne was an irreversible process. This was a law, abided by since ancient times. And so… if Prince Jeord really did relinquish his claim, reality would not change even if I were to reveal my sins at a later time.

That was why… when this all ended, as long as I had been of some assistance to Prince Ian, I had long since resigned myself to my future life as a prisoner and a sinner.

"Wh-Why? You're just trying to do something for Prince Ian, right? But now you're planning on calling off your engagement with him and turning yourself in? Is that really what you want?" Lady Katarina asked, the surprise plain in her voice.

"Yes… I was the one who started admiring Prince Ian in the first place. And now I have made up my mind. I am resolved," I answered without hesitation.

"Huh? But aren't you two engaged?"

My chest ached at Lady Katarina's words. That's right… I was still Prince Ian's fiancée as of now. But I explained the circumstances, how I was selected as Prince Ian's fiancée when we were young, but had proved to be a failure at both magic and academics. I described how my family began to believe that he should find a better fiancée, and how I had realized that I was holding Prince Ian back with my shortcomings.

I was sure that a more fitting fiancée would be found for Prince Ian soon enough. "Also… Prince Ian himself has nothing but contempt for me, so…"

I hardly ever saw him. Even when we did see each other, he did not seem very fond of me. That was why everyone said that Prince Ian disliked his fiancée. But of course... unlike the other princes' fiancées, he had to contend with me, useless as I was. It was all but impossible for him to like me.

Even so, I wanted to be useful to Prince Ian. Even if he hated me, and had nothing but contempt for me. I... I still loved him...

Lady Katarina stared at me for a while before finally starting to speak. "Well... Have you ever heard Prince Ian himself say that to you...?"

"Huh?" I was surprised at those words. I had never thought of such a thing before.

"Have you ever asked Prince Ian how he truly feels about you?"

"Th-There is no way I could ask him something like that! But then... everyone around me always talks about how Prince Ian is tired of me, how he dislikes me... and how he... already hates me..." After all, that was what everyone else said. They couldn't be wrong. So why? What was Lady Katarina saying?

"But Lady Selena... those are the words of other people, right? Have you heard the prince himself say it? Maybe you're just imagining that he hates you?"

"But..." This was something I had never thought about until now. I was terribly confused. *Is it just my imagination, then? That Prince Ian isn't fond of me? Are all those voices... wrong?*

"Someone's emotions can only be known by that person themselves, right? So, Lady Selena... if you wish to know the truth, you have to ask Prince Ian, and that's that!"

"Ask...?"

"Yes, speak to Prince Ian about it, or at least try!"

I won't know his true feelings on the matter if I don't ask...? I should... speak with Prince Ian? Can I really do such a thing? Is it okay for someone like me to...?

I raised my head and found Lady Katarina's her azure eyes staring straight into me.

"Say... Lady Selena. You've been saying that you were no good, that you are lacking, just now... and I don't think that's true. More importantly, you were worried about me, a complete stranger. You were worried if I could sleep. And you even have the resolve to get captured and sentenced... all in the name of helping someone you love," Lady Katarina said, with the gentlest gaze. "To me, Lady Selena, you are gentle and strong. There's not a single bone in you that is lacking or no-good. I think you are a wonderful person."

I am not lacking or no-good... I am... a wonderful person? "... That's the... first time... anyone has said anything like that to me..." I muttered, stunned.

I had been called useless and deficient up until now. Praises were rare, if I ever received them at all. Even if someone did praise me, it felt like nothing more than a pleasantry — the socially correct thing to say.

However... Lady Katarina was not lying. I knew this. Her piercing, honest gaze did not contain a single shred of malice or falsehood. Slowly, I felt the warmth of her words spread through my entire being.

"Well then! I'll keep saying it from here on out. As many times as you'd like. So... would you like to be friends, Lady Selena?"

I could only look on blankly at Lady Katarina's outstretched hand. *Ahh... perhaps this person before me really is a saint.*

"...To say such words towards one who kidnapped you... Lady Katarina, you truly are as the rumors say."

I felt a fire in my chest. I felt that… if I took her hand, something would change.

"…Even though I have done such a thing… I would like to be friends…" Saying so, I held Lady Katarina's hand in mine. Her hand was warm. "Lady Katarina… As you said, I won't be swayed by what others say anymore. I will speak with Prince Ian himself and hear what he has to say."

I had never thought of it that way. No one had ever said anything like this to me. Even if I did have such thoughts, I would surely be paralyzed by fear. I would have remained stuck in place, ruminating endlessly on the what-ifs.

But… now, I felt like I could do it. I felt a sense of strength flow into me from Lady Katarina's hand straight into mine.

"Yes, that's a good start!" Lady Katarina was still looking straight at me.

"…Yes." In a single breath, I felt all my hesitations evaporate. I nodded earnestly.

This girl, who was loved by everyone, was known as a saint. She was a mysterious person. It was almost as if a strange power dwelt in her words and in her sincere, unwavering gaze.

"But before that… I really need to stop this foolish kidnapping affair… and also atone for my sins…" That was where I would start, even if it meant that my engagement with Prince Ian would be broken off. Even so… if I spoke with Prince Ian personally, just like Lady Katarina suggested, then surely something would change.

"If it ever comes down to it, I'll keep it a secret!"

The saint was truly a compassionate person indeed. But I could not accept such an offer. I knew that I must take responsibility. I would atone for my sins, and speak with Prince Ian.

"Well then… I shall see to it that you are safely delivered back to Prince Jeord this instant. I shall begin making the preparations…" I headed towards the door.

The painful, binding sensation in my chest was gone. Now… I felt like I could do anything.

Just when I had finally found out the motive behind my kidnapping and made friends with Selena... that butler appeared. The young man by the name of Rufus, the butler who was always by Selena's side.

He had appeared out of nowhere and revealed some disturbing things. He claimed that Selena would be used as a scapegoat for the kidnapping plot, that she would disappear with Prince Ian, and that I would disappear with Jeord as well.

I was stunned, and for a while I just stood there, dumbstruck. Before I realized it, he had already left the room with the unconscious Selena in his arms. By the time I got a hold of myself and decided to chase after him, the door to my room was locked again, and I was left alone.

It was now late into the night. But of course, even I couldn't rest my mind in a situation like this. I couldn't stop thinking about what Rufus had said.

And Selena had collapsed and fallen to the ground... *"Just letting her sleep for a while,"* he'd said. But the way she had fallen asleep was nothing like how I'd been made to pass out at the school festival. He hadn't knocked her unconscious or anything like that. There was nothing — Selena simply collapsed quietly, just like that.

Rufus claimed that it was his doing, yet I didn't see him use any kind of drug or brute force. He just placed a hand on her shoulder. The power to put someone to sleep just by touching them... I only knew of one thing that matched that description.

It was a power I had learned about last year. The Dark Arts, magic that was only usable by Wielders of Darkness. The forbidden magic that was capable of manipulating the hearts and minds of others.

As soon as I asked Selena about the reason behind my kidnapping, that man would always interrupt us. She would then immediately fall silent, and her expression would go blank like a doll's.

I had a hunch. If my assumptions were correct, then that man, Rufus, was a Wielder of Darkness.

Dark Magic could technically be obtained by anyone as long as they were born with the ability to use magic. However, a ritual and a sacrifice were required, and said sacrifice was... the life of another human being.

Dark Magic was capable of controlling the emotions of others, but also of taking their lives. It was taboo, and its very existence was hidden from the general public.

If Rufus really was a Wielder of Darkness, then he must have gained his abilities through the ritual sacrifice. That meant that he was entirely capable of murder.

Of course, it could have been forced upon him, like how it had been with Raphael. But... the way he looked at the fallen Selena with those cold eyes, and the way he smiled, as if he were enjoying himself... Thinking about it made shivers run down my spine.

I'd thought that I would be completely unable to sleep, but I ended up drifting off and slumbering through the night.

Come to think of it, I had slept equally well on the night before the graduation ceremony, which is when all the Catastrophic Bad Ends could have occurred. So really, I guess I was able to sleep well at any given time or situation. I surprised even myself with my sleeping skills, especially after I'd been directly threatened by my kidnapper. He had said that I would "disappear."

And of course, the one who woke me from my deep sleep was none other than...

"Unbelievable... After everything that happened, you're just sleeping here? Does this chick have nerves of steel or something?!" It was an exasperated voice from someone near me. It sounded very frustrated.

"Hnnh?" *I was having such a good rest, too! What's with all the ruckus?* I thought. As I slowly opened my eyes, a man I recognized came into view. I saw him last night, I think. His name was... "Rufus...?"

"I am honored that you would remember the name of one such as myself, Lady Katarina. I do think, however, that it would be a most prudent time to rise. It is already past noon."

For some reason, he sounded very different than when I was still half asleep. But my ears didn't betray me — it was the same voice. *Then... I suppose he's the one who woke me up. More importantly, though...*

"Huh?! Already past noon!"

"...You react to that of all things, huh," Rufus said, once again sounding exasperated.

But… I only slept for a short while! Or at least, that's what I meant to do… In fact, I'd decided to stay up after Rufus had left and come up with a plan through the night! I was thinking that I could climb down the window in the darkness and escape. And yet here I was, sleeping past noon! And to make things worse, the antagonist of this entire situation had just woken me up!

"I do surprise myself sometimes, yes…" I admitted.

"…Well, I would be the surprised party, you see. I had not heard a thing from your room after all this time, and had assumed that you were simply hugging your knees and softly sobbing in a corner. To think that you would be sprawled out, spread-eagled, snoring on your bed…"

I could feel the sheer disbelief in his voice. *I see. So I was sleeping like that? That's so embarrassing…* But now wasn't the time to be concerned about that! I had to figure things out.

"There's a lot I want to ask you, but most importantly… is Selena alright?" Selena had suddenly collapsed, and was taken away. Was she safe? I stared straight at Rufus combatively, demanding an answer.

"…The rumors do not do you justice, do they? Very well, I shall answer your question. Lady Selena is fine; she is safely sleeping in her room."

"…Is that so." I had been staring at him all this time, but I couldn't tell if he was lying. I decided I'd believe him for now.

But like… more rumors? Really? Are they about me being spirited? Sassy? Like Selena was talking about?

And there was another point that I needed to confirm. "Rufus… are you a Wielder of Darkness?"

His eyes opened slightly at my question, but only one corner of his lip curled up in response. "… My, aren't you blunt with your questions."

Well yes. Blunt, even for me, but I was never good at extracting information from people with all sorts of fancy leading questions. "I couldn't think of any roundabout ways to ask, so…"

"What a strange person you are, indeed! Since you know of the existence of Dark Magic… well then. I suppose you, too, were involved in last year's incident."

"Oh!" I was shocked. Although news of the wrongdoing by a certain heir of a Marquess family had spread through noble circles, the fact that Dark Magic was involved should have been kept a secret.

Rufus continued on, as if reading my thoughts. "Surprised? Since that was supposed to be all hushed up… ah. But you see, it is impossible to cover everything up. After all, many nobles with close ties to the Dieke family are quite shady individuals themselves."

Rufus allowed a crooked smile to creep into his face as he made his declarations. "So you see… he, too, became interested in Dark Magic."

"…Him who?"

"Ah. That would be my master. I became a Wielder of Darkness under his orders, before making my way into the family of Duke Berg…"

"Wh-Why though?" I asked, still trying to aggressively extract information from the somewhat changed Rufus.

"Did I not just explain? So that Lady Selena could become the scapegoat for all these kidnappings and other assorted sins. So that she would disappear with Prince Ian, vanishing from the struggle for the throne, and eventually noble society altogether. The same goes for you and Prince Jeord, as well."

"Why would you do such a thing…?"

"Why? Because you are in the way, of course. I am working on behalf of the first prince, you see. Prince Jeffrey desires the throne…

and he is the kind of individual that would not hesitate to resort to various means to achieve his goals."

So Prince Jeffrey wanted the throne... Ian and Jeord were simply in his way? What about Alan, then? It was a serious conversation, and there were so many things I needed to think about. But from the corner of my mind came a soft complaint from Alan: *"Why am I the only one not included, huh?!"*

"Ah, it's okay, Alan. You're still growing," I thought, mentally comforting the discontent Alan in my mind.

Rufus, however, seemed to interpret my silence differently. "Surely even you are terrified now? Well then, I suppose that is all we need to talk about, now. I've left a light meal here — do help yourself." With that, Rufus left, but not before saying, "Well then, ring this bell if there is anything you need." With that, I was alone in the room once more.

I had slept a lot and wasn't tired anymore, so I supposed I should have that meal, for what it was worth. It was definitely on the light side, only consisting of a few types of small buns. *Honestly, this is nothing more than a snack for me!*

Still feeling somewhat let down by the small portion size, I grabbed a small, round bun off the tray and sank my teeth into it.

Wh-What? This... This is incredibly delicious! I'd sampled quite a few delicious buns and snacks at the festival stands not long ago, but the taste of this bun was wonderful — you couldn't even compare them. Its exterior was soft and tender, but its inner texture was chewy and delightful. *I could become addicted to these buns!*

And what is that, in the corner of the plate...? This cream... is it meant to go with the buns? I held the ridiculously delicious bun in my hand and dipped it in the cream.

Ooooh! This… This is truly amazing! While seeming like nothing more than custard cream at first glance, it's actually quite unique! This terribly sweet, yet refreshing, otherworldly taste! An incredible match for this bun.

Alright. Next up is this flatbread-like bun here…

Ah, this one was delicious, too. Just who was the person that made all these delicious morsels? I simply had to ask at the next chance I got.

And so, I finished the delicious bread in a matter of minutes. Now with some food in my stomach, it was time to seriously think about the details surrounding this kidnapping case.

"Slow as usual, huh," Alan's voice in my head said, but alas, what could I have done about it? I'd overslept.

Alright! We shall now commence an insightful analysis of the kidnap with a mental meeting.

Meeting chairwoman: Katarina Claes.

Meeting representative: Katarina Claes.

Meeting secretary: Katarina Claes.

"Well then, I do think we should begin by sorting out the facts of our current situation. I would like to hear everyone's opinions on the matter."

"Yes, if I may. Perhaps we should start our deductions by organizing what we heard from Selena last night, as well as what Rufus said."

"Yes, very much so. A good idea."

"I agree."

"Well then… from what Selena said yesterday, she's been depressed all this time, thinking that she was of no use to Prince Ian."

167

"That's right."

"And then this playboy butler, Rufus, appears at Selena's side, proposing to kidnap Katarina so that she may be useful to Prince Ian... are the facts straight so far?"

"Hmm... If that really is the case, then perhaps he used the Dark Arts on Selena..."

"And then, Selena, obediently following Rufus' plan, kidnaps Katarina. However, Rufus' true goal is to pin all of this on Selena — she would be the scapegoat, and this would lead to her and Prince Ian's downfall... correct?"

"Oh, Miss Katarina Claes, what skillful, acute clarity! More so than usual — did something special happen?"

"Heheheh. You see, I had some delicious bread and a good night's rest. My mind is now clearer and sharper than it has ever been, breaking all known barriers."

"That's amazing! As you are now, Miss Claes, you could start calling yourself Great Detective Katarina!"

"Oh, I like the sound of that. Great Detective Katarina... And soon after, I will open the Katarina Detective Agency, solving one impossible case after the other..."

"Everyone, please focus! This conversation is getting derailed!"

"Apologies..."

"Alright, back to the topic at hand... from what Rufus said, his master was the one who had instigated this entire kidnapping affair... and this is all to clear a path to the throne for Prince Jeffrey."

"That's what he said, yes."

"In that case, is the true mastermind behind all this Prince Jeffrey himself?"

"But then... I can't see him doing such a thing, especially after meeting him at the school festival."

"...Yes, and even the treats he brought were delicious."

"Ah yes, they were delectable."

"Yes, I would love to try them again! Ah, just thinking about it makes me hungry..."

"Honestly, that bread was delicious, but there wasn't quite enough of it!"

"Well said! That small portion size... enough for feeding the birds, maybe! Ugh! The conversation is getting derailed once more! We have to get back on track..."

"You say that, but... I've already used my head quite enough! Now I'm hungry, and I can't think about anything but food!"

"I feel the same way. After all, we don't think very often, do we? The brain of Katarina Claes is already at its limits. It thirsts for sugar!"

"...It is as you say. All I can see in my mind are images of food...! Bread, meat, fish..."

"...Cakes, cookies, pies..."

"...Apples, oranges, grapes..."

And so, the Katarinas started talking about food and nothing else. The meeting was forcibly aborted.

I can't do this anymore! All I see in my mind is food!

I know! I'll have something brought to me.

With that, I leapt up, swiftly ringing the bell that Rufus had left me.

"...No way. Just how cocky can you get? Is this chick even really a noble lady...?" Rufus muttered, in a tone somewhat different from the one I was used to, as he poured me a cup of tea.

When Rufus arrived after I rang the bell, he'd said, "Oh, what have we here? Even the great Lady Katarina is uneasy, now? However, your role is to remain here just for a little while longer..." He spoke with a villainous smile on his face.

My response was simple: "Oh nah, nothing like that. I'm hungry, actually. Please give me something to eat. It'll be tea time soon, right? I'd appreciate some sweets and tea."

Rufus froze at my words. For a while, he remained unmoving... before a loud, audible rumble rose up from the depths of my stomach. The sound was enough to knock him back to his senses.

He left the room and then returned with a small cart laden with tea and snacks. Although he did seem somewhat scary a few moments ago, he did listen to my request and brought me the food and drink I asked for. Maybe he wasn't such a bad person after all.

"Well, here it is. Enjoy," he said, handing me a cup of tea as he did so.

Thanking him, I took the cup in my hands. "Could I ask that you join me for tea? I don't really like to have it by myself," I said. It was true; my friends usually had tea with me. Even the previous day, Lana had accompanied me.

I figured it was fair to ask Rufus to join me this time around. He did bring me food, after all. Surely this wouldn't be too much to ask? So I thought, but I was merely faced with another empty expression of surprise. *Rufus really likes this expression, huh?*

"...You... really... Ah, whatever. There'll be no end to this craziness if I keep on getting surprised." Rufus sat down across from me, a cup in one hand.

Hmm... So I guess he's not a bad person after all, just as I thought. One thing was bothering me, though.

"Did the way you speak just... change?" Although I had spoken to Rufus somewhat freely, he had always addressed me formally, like earlier in the morn... well, noon. But now, he was speaking very casually.

"Ah that, yeah. I had to play the part of the butler and stuff, so I had to talk that way. But dealing with someone like you and keeping that up at the same time is kind of a pain in the ass, you know? That's why I've gone back to talking like I normally do. I could revert to my former way of speaking if it causes you distress, my lady."

That final statement sounded unnatural, and was accompanied by an artificial smile. Now, more than ever, I could feel the dissonance.

"No, this is fine. Having you go back to talking formally feels kind of... wrong."

"Ha, you think?"

"But so... you said you were playing the role of a butler? So you never really were one?"

Now that I was talking to him in this way, Rufus seemed like a typical guy from a downtown district. And yet he'd looked more butler-like than Sebastian, the Claes family butler, when I first met him...

"Do I look like a butler to you now?"

"Not really, no. No matter how I look at you now, you just seem like a young man from some downtown district in a nearby city." I felt that I should offer a simple, honest answer.

"Not bad! You're spot on. Pretty good," Rufus replied, seemingly impressed. "Actually... you're a noble, right? And you go downtown?"

"...Sometimes. I dress up and look the part." I actually dragged Keith along and went pretty often. The food was cheap, there was fun to be had around every corner, and more than anything else, I liked the feeling of being a simple commoner.

That was, of course, all a secret. If Mother knew about it, she would be so upset and would start telling me off for "wandering off and fooling around again."

"But then… you really are just an average guy from a downtown district? Were you born there?"

"Well, no. You got it right, mostly, but I wasn't born there. My social life was spent there, yes, but I was born in the slums."

"Huh? Slums! There are slums in this kingdom?!"

I understood what the word meant. But the kingdom that I lived in did pretty well for itself, mainly due to many of its population being gifted with magic. Even the commoners of these lands lived better than those in surrounding kingdoms and countries. So I'd been taught that slums didn't exist… Did I simply not know of them?

Rufus, however, quickly dispelled any doubts I had. "Ah, you got it all wrong. I wasn't born in this kingdom."

"Oh, is that right?" *So would this make Rufus a foreigner?* I wondered. I couldn't tell just by looking at him. To me, he didn't seem foreign at all.

"When I was a kid, I was playing around with my friends from the slums when I got caught by human traffickers. So I got sold, and wandered from place to place until I was bought by my current master… in this country."

Although his words were overwhelmingly casual, the reality behind them was not, and for a while I found myself at a loss for words.

"Surprised? A noble raised with love and care probably won't believe this, but it's more common than you think, you know? Especially in poorer countries. If anything, I'm lucky, right? I still have all my limbs, I'm still alive, and now I have these fine clothes to wear. I'm blessed, you know?" Rufus said, as his eyes gazed off into the distance — at some faraway place beyond the confines of this room.

Some kind of feeling was rising up in my chest as I watched him. I wondered what it was…

"Ha, cat got your tongue? Even you are silent now. Or are you pitying me, thinking this is all really sad? Sorry, but I don't need any of that. I don't think of myself as unfortunate." The corner of Rufus' lip curled up once more. His blue eyes stared right at me. It didn't seem like he was putting up a brave front.

I finally started to understand what the feeling welling up in my chest was. "…cool."

"Huh?" It seemed that Rufus hadn't heard what I said, at least not clearly enough. I repeated myself.

"I think you're pretty cool, Rufus."

"…What's this all of a sudden? Well, I get that I don't look too shabby, but…"

"No, I'm not talking about how you look, but how you are on the inside. How you think."

"…The hell is that supposed to mean? I don't get it at all."

"The straightforward way you think… I think it's impressive. And cool."

There were many in both common and noble society who blamed their own misfortunes on others. They would go on about how unfortunate they were, and how they had such a hard life, and should be pitied… and so on.

Although he had gone through so much in his life, Rufus didn't seem to bemoan his own circumstances. In fact, he claimed that he was blessed — and this was what made me think that he was cool.

As I continued looking at him with an admiring gaze, Rufus froze up once more. *Huh? What happened? Did I say something rude?* Now that I calmly thought about it, I supposed I should have said something along the lines of "I empathize."

"...Can't believe it. I'm all the way here, and I've met someone who says exactly the same stuff that guy did...?" Rufus remained frozen for a while, before a small, but visible shiver set into his shoulders.

This is bad! I must have said something rude, and now Rufus is shivering in anger!

The tension was soon interrupted by a loud guffaw, however, and before I knew it, Rufus was hugging his stomach, laughing thunderously. His laughter was explosive, to say the least.

Huh? Why? What was funny about what I said? I could only continue to ponder as I waited for Rufus to calm down.

After a while, he finally recovered from his laughing fit and spoke again. "Ha... You're really interesting, you know that? Been a while since I laughed like this."

"Huh..." I didn't remember saying anything particularly funny.

"Hey, let's talk some more. I suddenly feel like it'd be good to keep talking."

"...Huh."

After that, I talked to Rufus at length...

...about the delicious bread in that light meal.

"So, please do tell! The bread in that light meal you offered me just now... who made it?"

"Ah, that? I bought it from that one bakery downtown, you know? Though I believed it would not fit the tastes of a lady—"

"Huh?! A bakery downtown? Where exactly is it? It was so delicious! I really must go and buy some next time!"

"You're really weird, you know that?"

…and about my hobbies and skills.

"Tilling fields is one of my hobbies!"

"Fields? Like… flower fields? Something like that?"

"Nope. Fields with crops."

"…Why?"

"Why? Well, because it's fun, I suppose?"

"…"

"Oh, and I'm the top when it comes to tree-climbing and fishing skills! I'm pretty confident about it!"

"…Are you even really a noble lady?"

…and about stories of the foreign lands Rufus had seen before ending up in this kingdom.

"Say, you said you've wandered from place to place, right? How many kingdoms and foreign lands have you been to?"

"How many…? A bunch, here and there, I guess?"

"Which kingdoms have you been to? I want to hear more about other kingdoms besides this one!"

"Sure, but I don't think it's gonna be anything pretty, if you're expecting something like that. After all, all I've done is wander through the dirty underbellies of a bunch of societies… Still want to hear about it?"

"Underbelly! Societies! So it's a hardboiled world!"

"Huh? Hard what? And… why are your eyes sparkling like that? Just what are you expecting…?"

Rufus had lots of stories about places and events that I'd never heard of before. It was very interesting. I wanted to hear more and more, but most of the day went by before I even realized it.

"So… come to think of it, since you're not really a butler, does that mean that 'Rufus' is a false name, too?" I asked, the thought suddenly crossing my mind.

"Yeah, I used the Dark Arts to infiltrate the Berg family and all that, you know? So what would be the point in using my actual name?" That made sense.

"Well then… what's your real name?"

"I have more names than I can count. One for each place, you know?"

Ooohh! As expected of one who's lived in the underbellies of societies, a true hardboiled life!

"Then what was your original name?" I asked, leaning in as I did so.

Before I realized it, Rufus' face was right in front of me. *Ooh.* This is the first time I'd seen his face up close. Now that I was at this distance… *Hmm, he has very sensual features…*

"Don't got one. Unlike you lot, I don't have parents. By the time I even thought about who I was, I was already sifting through trash in the slums."

Ooh, he even has a beauty spot under one of his eyes — one of the prerequisite features for a sensual, flirty character. It truly was something else. This man, laden with sex appeal, far exceeded Keith's capabilities. And then there were his eyes, behind the lenses of his glasses…

"Oi! What's with you, clamming up like that? Too traumatic of a conversation for a lady like yourself?"

"…really beautiful."

"Huh?"

"Your eyes! Your eyes are really beautiful, like the pure blue sky!"

"…"

Now that I was this close, Rufus' eyes were indeed a clear shade of blue, like the skies above on a good day. The way the setting sun lit up his eyes — it was almost like they were sparkling. Anyone would fall for that.

"…You really…"

"Hm?"

Rufus extended his hand, placing it on my cheek. The touch of his pretty fingers was somewhat ticklish. *Is there something stuck on my cheek? Food, maybe?*

Also, why is his face slowly approaching mine? Am I simply imagining things?

A familiar sound rose from my belly at that exact moment; the thunderous roar of hunger.

Although I had been fed sweets and snacks earlier, it was already evening, and my stomach was informing me of the current time of day. It was dinner time.

Rufus' movements stopped at the loud sound, and suddenly his shoulders were shivering again.

After a while, the shivering stopped, and with a simple laugh, he said, "Guess I'll bring you dinner too, huh."

Although I'd been moved to a separate room to have my dinner yesterday, it seemed like I'd be having it in this room tonight. At Rufus' command, the servants who'd brought me my meals yesterday started bringing dinner into the room.

As usual, I didn't like eating alone. I invited Rufus, and he was quick to agree.

"Come to think of it, what happened to Lana? I haven't seen her…"

Everything that Lana had done for me yesterday was now being handled by Rufus, it seemed. I hadn't seen her since she'd guided Selena into my room last night.

"Ah, I have her working on some other things. Don't worry about that."

Is that so? That's good, then. I did want to speak more with her, though.

Soon after, I started asking Rufus about his time in foreign lands again. Homes and villages made entirely of stone, a city with a river flowing through it, with its residents commuting with the aid of boats and ships... Rufus regaled me with tales of his time there, and the work he did. It was all very thrilling and interesting.

"Ha! Honestly Rufus, your stories are so interesting."

"The things you tell me are interesting too. It's too bad you're some nobleman's daughter."

This was a compliment, right? I chose to believe so, saying a plain "thank you" and nodding my head. "I've never set foot outside this kingdom, but when I'm talking to you, it feels like I've gone on an overseas vacation!"

My previous life did end without me taking a single step out of Japan, after all. If possible, I wanted to visit other countries in this new life of mine.

"Haha, well if it's with you, I feel like I'd like to go visit those places again."

"Oh!" My father was overprotective, and Mother didn't really like me going out very much. I once asked why, only for her to say that *"The shame would eventually find its way back to me."* I didn't really get it.

Considering all that, visiting a foreign country was like a dream within a dream. Even so, I was ecstatic at Rufus' words.

"Really? Then please do take me with you next time!" I said, looking at him with sparkling, anticipatory eyes. Rufus, however, returned my gaze with a troubled expression.

Huh? Did I mess up? I really did believe what Rufus said... but maybe it was just well-intentioned flattery?

"We live in different worlds, you and me. You know that, right? There's no way I can take you with me." That was his response.

"Different... worlds? What do you mean? Aren't you sitting before me right now, as you are?"

"..."

"We're talking together, eating together. Doesn't this mean we're in the same world, then?"

What's he going on about? I shook my head slightly, before looking at Rufus once more — only to find him frozen in place... again? *Hmm? What is it this time?*

"You... really are a strange one, you know that? Okay, I get it. I'll bring you along next time."

Alright! Here's to my first vacation-friend! "Okay! It's a promise. Hm... let's pinky promise," I said, holding out my little finger. Rufus, however, didn't seem to understand the gesture.

Ah, right... those probably don't exist in this world. Hmm... how are promises made in this world again?

That's right! I headed to the drawer where the dress I had initially worn at the time I was captured was kept and stuck my hand into its pocket. *There it is!*

I held it tight and returned to Rufus' side. I then placed the item squarely in his hands. "Here. A symbol of our promise — I am entrusting it to you."

Although there was no such thing as pinky promises in this world, an equivalent did exist — and that was handing over a personal possession to the other person.

"This is a… brooch?" Rufus said, staring at the object in his hands.

It was a brooch indeed, the blue one that my classmates had encouraged me to buy. "It's a pretty color, right? It matches your eyes. The blue of the sky."

"…"

I retrieved the brooch from Rufus' outstretched hand. "And then… if you tilt it this way so that it catches the light… see? It's aqua-blue now. Like how my eyes are, right?"

With that, I returned the brooch to his hands once more. "The color of your eyes, and the color of mine… this brooch is both at the same time! Perfect as a symbol of our promise."

I personally thought it was an amazing suggestion, and was very proud of myself. Rufus, however, was making that familiar dumbstruck expression again.

Huh? What? Why? What happened? How mysterious, I thought.

Suddenly, I felt myself drawn in. Rufus had put his arm around me, bringing me close — and before I knew it, I found myself in his arms. In the very next moment, he had swept me off my feet, and he was now apparently carrying me entirely.

Hmm… I feel like you only see this kind of princess-carry in manga or games.

But huh? Why? I was at a loss as I found myself being transported to the room's bed, before Rufus promptly placed me down on it.

"Being with you… warms me up, you know. Been a while since I felt anything like this."

Huh? What's with this position? My back was now squarely on the bed, and Rufus was looking down at me from above.

At some point in time, the glasses he wore had come off as well, and I was able to get a much better view of his blue eyes now that the lenses were out of the way.

Ahh… he really does have pretty eyes. They were so beautiful that I forgot this strange situation in an instant.

"Hey… would you like to be mine?" His pure blue eyes were such a wonderful color. "If you keep looking at me with your eyes sparkling like that… don't complain if I end up doing… something," Rufus said, bringing his head close to my neck. The sound of his breaths finally jolted me back to reality.

Wh-What is this situation… no! It can't be! Placing me on the bed like that… he's going to use the Dark Arts on me and put me to sleep!

I'd let my guard down, thinking he was a nice person, but it didn't change the fact that he was responsible for my kidnap in the first place! He even said that he would have me disappear… at this rate, I'd be put to sleep for multiple days!

While my two-day magic-induced slumber last year was quite refreshing, it was hard on my body when I did wake up! If I was put to sleep again for two days, that would be fine, but a few weeks… the mere thought of the ensuing muscle pains was enough to worry me.

"Um… wait— Rufus…?" A slight spike of pain spread through my neck as I opened my mouth to speak. For some reason, I felt like I had experienced this before… what was it, again? Was I being bitten by a bug, perhaps? Just as the pain was about to steal away my consciousness once more…

Bang bang! Two loud thuds came from the direction of the door, followed by Lana's loud voice. "Master Rufus, are you available?"

Rufus clicked his tongue softly at her words. "I am currently occupied."

But Lana wasn't so easily driven away. "It is quite an urgent matter," came her response, in the same loud voice.

In the end, Rufus gave in, climbing off the bed and heading towards the door. "Ugh... right when it was getting good, too," Rufus sighed before opening the door.

Lana greeted him with a smile. "A letter of utmost importance has just arrived for you," she said.

"From whom...?" Rufus said, seemingly displeased.

Lana's smile, however, didn't waver. "I have left it in your room. Perhaps it would be in your interest to read it as soon as possible."

Rufus' eyes opened wide at Lana's statement. "...You. No... can't be. Well. I guess that's how it is..." He sighed heavily before exiting the room altogether.

Lana rushed in soon after. "Lady Katarina, are you alright?" she asked, worry evident on her face.

"I'm okay. I thought he was about to cast magic on me..."

"Ah? Magic? Where?"

"Hmm? Ah, he had pinned me down on the bed, and I was sure he was going to use his magic to put me to sleep... But I was saved thanks to you, Lana!"

"..."

Huh? What is it now? Lana had an unreadable expression on her face.

"Well... in any case. I am very glad you are alright," Lana said, before sighing deeply for some reason.

There were many things I didn't understand, but I found myself in the bed once more on the second night of my confinement.

I'd assumed that I would have trouble sleeping, given that I had overslept well into the noon. But I ended up falling asleep with no trouble at all. *Truly amazing, Katarina Claes!*

However… yet another visitor came knocking in the night.

"Katarina… psst. Katarina."

"Huh…?" Still half asleep, I turned my eyes to the source of the voice… only to see Rufus standing at my bedside.

"Wah!" I gasped, involuntarily jumping out of my sheets.

"Haha. You really do sleep well, huh."

"Wh-What do you want?" I asked in a more guarded fashion, remembering what had happened after our dinner.

"I guess I really put you on your guard, huh. But that's fine. I won't be doing anything anymore. It's time to face the music."

"Face… music?"

"Yeah. To tell the truth, I wanted to escape with you, out of this kingdom… but I guess that would be too reckless. I'll give up on that. It's all become very complicated, see, because of this magic. Seems like I have to be good for a while… and be taken into custody."

"Wha?" *Hmm?* I didn't understand what he was saying. *What's this all about? Flee the kingdom? Custody?*

"Well… I guess I'll never see you again if I go along with it, so I'm here. Hoping to see your face one last time."

With that, he extended his arm once more and placed his hand on my face. His touch was ticklish, like before.

"One last time? What do…"

Before I could ask him what this was all about, I could suddenly hear a series of sounds outside.

"Oh… they're faster than I expected." Rufus withdrew his hand and retreated some distance away from my bedside.

At that very moment, the door was thrown open with a loud slam, and before me was none other than…

"Huh…? Why is everyone here?"

Jeord, Keith, Mary, Alan, Sophia, Nicol, Maria, and Raphael. All of my friends rushed into the room, their expressions all grave and severe. Leading them all was…

"…Lana?"

"Yes. I introduced myself as such a while ago, but I suppose re-introductions are in order. I am Larna Smith, of the Magical Ministry. Raphael's boss. Nice to meet you."

"Huh?!" *Isn't she a maid? What was this? She's Raphael's boss at the Ministry?*

She regarded me with a smile as I remained stunned. Then she shifted her gaze to Rufus. "I see that you have chosen to remain… have you steeled yourself for what is to come, then?"

"Yes. I'll tell you everything… in your custody," Rufus said, nodding meekly. His expression didn't seem authentic, though.

"Well said. I see your head is in the right place. Without further ado… Rufus Brode. You are hereby under arrest for the kidnap of Lady Katarina Claes. Well then, take him away."

At Lana's, or I guess, Larna's command, some people stepped out from behind her — staff members of the Ministry, probably. They surrounded Rufus swiftly. Before long, he was restrained and led out of the room.

What is this feeling…? I had been on guard after realizing that he had attempted to use his magic on me… But the way he lived his life was cool, and his stories were interesting. I felt uneasiness well up in my chest.

"U-Um!"

Rufus and his entourage of Ministry guards stopped at the sound of my voice. But… I was at a loss for words. What did I want to say, exactly…?

And then — "I'll hold onto it. Until our promise is fulfilled," Rufus said, opening his palm ever so slightly. My eyes caught a gleam of blue. It was the brooch that I had given to him.

I could only nod and respond cheerfully with a simple "Yes!"

With that, Rufus was taken away to the Magical Ministry.

★★★★★★★★★★

By the time I even thought about who I was, I was already living with my friends in the slums. I stole, cheated, and lied — it was the most obvious thing to do. I had no parents, no name. My friends in the slums taught me their way of life.

But everything changed when a certain man came to our territory.

He came from the outside world. Looked lanky, almost, but was surprisingly powerful. Before I knew it, he was already living close to us.

The man was different — he had a name. I learned a lot from him.

Many kids in my group didn't like this man from the outside world. But I thought that the things he had to say were interesting, so I quickly got to know him.

And then one day… this man gave me, a slum rat, a name. He called me "Sora." I asked him where it came from.

"From your beautiful blue eyes; like the sky," the man said, laughing as he gazed at my eyes. I felt a strange warmth welling up in my chest. It was like nothing I'd ever felt before.

From that day, I began calling myself Sora, and started visiting this man even more than before. He had a lot more than just stories of the outside world — he even taught me how to read and write, and also basic math. The boundaries of my world expanded because of him. Before I realized it, each day was becoming happier than the last.

One day, the man said to me, "Hey, Sora. Don't you dislike the things I tell you about the outside world?"

"What kinda question is that?"

"Well, you see... the rest of them don't like hearing about it. They all end up feeling miserable. You are the only one who doesn't react that way."

"Why miserable?"

"...Well. It's that... upon knowing of the outside world, they become aware of their own situation, you see?"

"I don't get it. What's that mean?"

"...That is to say. You all don't even have names, and struggle to live from day to day. Doesn't it feel bad to hear stories of children in the outside world, who are loved and cherished by their parents?"

"Ah... so that's what you mean."

"You don't feel miserable when hearing about things like that?"

"Hmm... I mean, people from the outside world are just that, right? They're people from the outside world, and I'm just me. It's none of my business how a bunch of people I don't know live their lives."

"…Are you not dissatisfied with your current way of life, Sora?"

"'Course I am! Even I want to sleep in a nice warm bed and eat a good meal! Even so, what are you gonna do about it? Being envious of some other people you don't know doesn't really help. You know… I don't really think of myself as unfortunate or anything. After all, I'm living safely every day, and I can talk about these interesting things with you, right? I think that's enough for me."

"…You know Sora, you're pretty cool."

"Wh-What are you saying, out of nowhere! You messing with me?"

"Ha! Hardly. I just feel that the way you think is really admirable. It's cool. You should keep living your life just as you are… without ever being swept away by those around you." The man placed a hand on my head, ruffling my hair. For some reason, I felt my cheeks heat up.

It was a while after this exchange that the man fell very, very ill. Although he was strong, I guess his body couldn't keep up with the dirty living conditions of the slums.

The man grew weaker and weaker with each passing day. My other friends all said the same thing. That nothing could be done, that this was something that happened a lot to people who wander into the slums… that I should just give up. But I didn't give up.

Up until then, I had seen so many of my friends die from sickness, or wounds that never quite healed… but I just couldn't give up on the man.

And so… I eventually sneaked into a house on my own. A house belonging to a family with a high social standing. And then I was caught, and sold to slavers. I don't know what happened to the man after that.

I drifted from country to country, kingdom to kingdom. I came to know of just how big the world was, and how ugly it could be. Thanks to the language and math skills the man taught me, I was of more use than most of the others from the slums. I was valued.

Even so… sometimes, I was just so disgusted. There were times when I wanted to shout at, scream at, hurl insults at the world. But whenever I felt that way, I remembered the man's words. *"I just feel that the way you think is really admirable. It's cool. You should keep living your life just as you are… without ever being swept away by those around you."*

They were the words of a man who was gone from this world… and yet, they stayed with me.

It was a few years ago when I ended up serving David Mason. Mason bought me for a reason — the fact that I could use magic. Though I couldn't really do much; maybe just start a small fire, but that was it.

Back in the slums, my bed was always under the cold, wintery skies. My powers were useful then, but I was surprised to find out that what I was doing had been a sign of magical talent. I had been mostly drifting through countries that didn't really have magic, and that's why no one noticed it for so long.

But Mason found out after buying me that I didn't have much magical power at all. He probably bought me thinking I was really strong, and wanted to use my powers.

So, even though I was bought for that exact reason, I didn't end up having much of a chance to use my magic at all. I ended up learning everything the other thugs and ruffians who were purchased with me were taught. All the different threats, backdoor dealings, and dirty deeds we helped him out with.

Still, it was a lot easier to live with Mason than it had been in the places I'd been before. We were taught the right social etiquette we needed for sneaking into different situations. There were hot meals every day, and a soft, comfortable bed to sleep in. And it got even better — we were given fine clothing, and we had all the women we wanted. It was just one good thing after the next.

After a while, I began thinking that this was it, that I could just continue living my life to the fullest here. But trouble had a way of finding me, and its tendrils soon creeped into my life.

It all began last year. It involved some Marquess' family, and apparently Dark Magic had been involved. Dark Magic could be used to control people. It was a taboo subject, or so I was told, but word of what had happened somehow got out into the world. Of course, information like that is usually erased by the powers that be, but that family had a lot of dark connections, so the news had leaked to even a small-time crook like Mason.

That was how I learned about Dark Magic, the Dark Arts, and how people got that kind of power. The power that Mason wanted. To get it, someone who could use magic had to perform a ritual that involved a sacrifice. That sacrifice was another person's life.

Mason, of course, didn't have any magic, and that was when he remembered that I existed. Under his orders, I would obtain Dark Magic.

And so... I underwent the ritual with a sacrifice Mason had prepared — an elderly person with no living relatives. Honestly, the idea of sacrificing someone to gain powers seemed very suspicious to me. In fact, I doubted that it would even work. But Mason, despite being a small-time crook, had actually done the work and received reliable information. As a result, I successfully gained the powers of the Dark Arts.

But when I actually tried using it, I realized that it wasn't as powerful as you might think. There were a lot of rules. For starters, it was impossible to make someone feel emotions that they didn't originally have. For instance, I couldn't make someone love something that they hated and vice versa.

And then there was the fact that my magical power was low to begin with. This is probably why my Dark Magic didn't work on people who were really strong in magic. If their magic was stronger than mine, it was hard for me to affect them. Mason was pretty irritated when he realized all this.

David Mason belonged to a political faction that supported the first prince of the kingdom, Jeffrey Stuart. He was probably promised a high position once Jeffrey became king, so he did everything he could to ensure that Jeffrey would take the throne. That was why he ordered me to become a Wielder of Darkness to begin with.

From what I understood, Mason had planned to have me use these powers on Prince Jeffrey's enemies. That'd be Prince Ian and Prince Jeord. I was supposed to make them renounce their claims to the throne, but the difference in magical power between me and them was too much. I knew it would be impossible to influence them. All of the princes were very magically talented, so even trying would be too much of a risk.

For a while, Mason was irritated and upset by the failure of his plans. He even took it out on me. But he calmed down after a while, and eventually decided to think of some way to utilize the Dark Magic he had. Well… I was the one who had it, but anyway.

Mason thought and thought about what to do. He wasn't very smart, but he finally came up with a plan… which was this kidnapping.

My target would not be Prince Ian at all, but his fiancée, Selena Berg. Apparently she didn't have very strong magical power at all. I would then use her to capture Prince Jeord's fiancée, Katarina Claes, who didn't have much magical talent either. With that done, the plan was to use the two as hostages and force the two princes to renounce their claims to the throne.

After everything was said and done, I would pin everything on Selena and erase the powerful Berg family from noble society. They were an important family that supported Prince Ian, and this would get them out of the way. At least, that was the plan.

Really though, David Mason wasn't a very smart man. I'd been to many places, and seen many types of criminals... but Mason? He was nothing more than a small-time crook. For him to come up with such a complicated plan... Well, he tried his best, but there were too many holes.

Still, if the plan were to fall through, all I had to do was cut all ties with him and escape. If I couldn't do that, all I had to say was that my master made me do it against my will, and probably shed some tears for effect. I was born with a pretty good face, I'd like to think. If I made an adequate expression of sorrow and cried a few tears, they'd immediately empathize with me. I had so many close calls in my life, and had overcome so many dangerous situations. It would be no different this time. It'd all work out, one way or another.

And so, I put on the expensive clothing that was prepared for me and put on some glasses to look the part, and infiltrated the Berg family home. After making my preparations, I successfully kidnapped Katarina Claes, but...

"Unbelievable… After everything that happened, you're just sleeping here? Does this chick have nerves of steel or something?!" I said, unintentionally reverting back to how I normally spoke.

It had been two days since Katarina was kidnapped. Last night, I had used the Dark Arts on Selena to make sure she wouldn't tell Katarina anything. But that night, Selena sneaked out when I wasn't watching. She crept into Katarina's room and ended up telling her everything about the kidnapping plot, before finally saying that she'd let her go, and that the kidnapping was over.

I guess Selena's will was stronger than I'd given her credit for, and the magic had been partly dispelled. I couldn't believe I made such a mistake… ugh. What a failure.

But of course, I couldn't just let things end like that, so I put Selena to sleep with my Dark Magic. And I made sure to issue a light threat to Katarina too while I was at it.

When I visited her room the next morning, I assumed that the silence was one of fear, and that she was curled up and cowering somewhere. But then, noon passed without a sound. *Did she pass out from the fear? This is why I don't like dealing with noble ladies…* At least, that's what I thought.

I entered her room — and lying spread-eagled before me was the sleeping Katarina. She was sleeping very well, from the looks of it. I couldn't stop myself from saying something about it. It was just too much.

"Hnnh? Rufus…?" I guess Katarina finally woke up, sensing that someone else was in the room. Then she called my name.

"I am honored that you would remember the name of one such as myself, Lady Katarina. I do think, however, that it would be a most prudent time to rise. It is already past noon," I said.

She was surprised. "Huh?! Already past noon!"

For a moment, I went back to my normal way of speaking from the absurdity of it all. "...You react to that of all things, huh."

"I do surprise myself sometimes, yes..."

"...Well, I would be the surprised party, you see. I had not heard a thing from your room after all this time, and had assumed that you were simply hugging your knees and softly sobbing in a corner. To think that you would be sprawled out, spread-eagled, snoring on your bed..."

Is she really the daughter of some noble? Maybe I kidnapped the wrong person by mistake? It was enough to make me start doubting myself.

The rumors all said that she was... kind of weird. But I didn't think she'd be quite *this* weird. At that point, I definitely thought she was a little crazy. Then she stared right at me and spoke.

"There's a lot I want to ask you, but most importantly... is Selena alright?"

She's the type that carves and walks her own path, huh. "...The rumors do not do you justice, do they? Very well, I shall answer your question. Lady Selena is fine; she is safely sleeping in her room."

"...Is that so." With that, she started staring at me again. "Rufus... are you a Wielder of Darkness?"

A surprisingly straightforward question. Even I was caught off guard by how forward she was. "...My, aren't you blunt with your questions."

"I couldn't think of any roundabout ways to ask, so..." Katarina responded, sounding absent-minded.

"What a strange person you are, indeed! Since you know of the existence of Dark Magic... well then. I suppose you, too, were involved in last year's incident."

She was surprised to hear that I knew about Dark Magic, but judging by how Selena had spilled the beans yesterday, I supposed it was fine to talk about it. All I had to do if it came down to it was to manipulate her memories. And since the threat yesterday seemed to have had no effect on this eccentric noble lady, I had to scare her a little more.

"So you see… he, too, became interested in Dark Magic."

"…Him who?"

"Ah. That would be my master. I became a Wielder of Darkness under his orders, before making my way into the family of Duke Berg…"

"Wh-Why though?"

"Did I not just explain? So that Lady Selena could become the scapegoat for all these kidnappings and other assorted sins. So that she would disappear with Prince Ian, vanishing from the struggle for the throne, and eventually noble society altogether. The same goes for you and Prince Jeord, as well."

"Why would you do such a thing…?"

"Why? Because you are in the way, of course. I am working on behalf of the first prince, you see. Prince Jeffrey desires the throne… and he is the kind of individual that would not hesitate to resort to various means to achieve his goals," I said, allowing a cold, heartless smile to flit across my lips. Katarina fell silent.

Finally! I've had some effect. At this rate, she would probably keep to herself from now on. With that, I left her the light meal I had brought and the bell to summon me. *Well, she'll probably never ring it anyway.* Or so I thought…

I realized how naive that thought was less than an hour later when I was surprised by the sound of the bell ringing. I thought she might be unnerved by my threats, but...

"Oh nah, nothing like that. I'm hungry, actually. Please give me something to eat. It'll be tea time soon, right? I'd appreciate some sweets and tea."

Katarina's brazen request completely changed what I thought of her. Before, I thought she was just an eccentric, but I was wrong. She was a total freak.

With that in mind... continuing the whole butler charade seemed stupid. After all, this girl probably didn't care how I spoke at all. I prepared the snacks and tea she'd asked for and handed them to her. With a simple "thank you," she quickly accepted.

A noble thanking a servant...? Katarina was either really off her rocker... or maybe she wasn't an arrogant noble at all.

After a single sip of the cup of tea, she said, "Could I ask that you join me for tea? I don't really like to have it by myself."

"...You... really... Ah, whatever. There'll be no end to this craziness if I keep on getting surprised." I really didn't have the energy to be surprised by this girl anymore. I sat down, just as she requested.

"Did the way you speak just... change?"

Ah. Guess she finally noticed. I explained that this was how I usually talked, when I wasn't playing the part of the butler. "I could revert to my former way of speaking if it causes you distress, my lady," I offered, meaning to give her a smile that was as fake as my last sentence, but then...

"No, this is fine. Having you go back to talking formally feels kind of... wrong," she declared casually.

"Ha, you think?"

"But so… you said you were playing the role of a butler? So you never really were one?"

Under normal circumstances, I would have simply evaded the question. But for some reason… I felt like I could talk about it with this girl.

"Do I look like a butler to you now?"

"Not really, no. No matter how I look at you now, you just seem like a young man from some downtown district in a nearby city."

"Not bad! You're spot on. Pretty good. Actually… you're a noble, right? And you go downtown?"

"…Sometimes. I dress up and look the part."

Her answer was honestly surprising. Most nobles looked down on the common people; they wouldn't be caught dead in a place like that. Mason was the same way. His eyes probably couldn't even see commoners. That was why he used us however he wanted, like disposable pawns.

…This girl was nothing like Mason. She was the oldest daughter of a Duke, and yet this high-class noble lady was going to a place like the downtown district. Just like the weirdo she was.

Katarina asked if I was born downtown, and I told her that I was born in the slums.

"Huh? Slums! There are slums in this kingdom?!"

Seemed like she misunderstood. I corrected her, saying, "Ah, you got it all wrong, see. I wasn't born in this kingdom."

"Oh, is that right?"

Katarina's surprised face made the mischievous part of my heart tingle.

I never thought of hiding the fact that I was raised in the slums. I didn't think it was a bad thing, but when I told people, they always furrowed their brows and looked at me like I was dirt. Either that, or they'd look at me with pity, especially if I talked about how I was raised.

But Katarina just seemed surprised. I wondered how she'd react if I told her a bit more about my life. With that in mind, I told her about how I had been picked up by human traffickers, and had wandered around before I was brought to my current master.

Katarina just looked more and more surprised. That reaction wasn't too different from most other people at this point. I went on.

"Surprised? A noble raised with love and care probably won't believe this, but it's more common than you think, you know? Especially in poorer countries. If anything, I'm lucky, right? I still have all my limbs, I'm still alive, and now I have these fine clothes to wear. I'm blessed, you know?"

As I talked, I couldn't help but start thinking of that man, the one who'd given me my name, for the first time in a while. That man probably wasn't alive anymore… but I think I said this same thing to him long ago.

I found myself getting a little nostalgic. Returning my attention back to Katarina, I noticed that she was now silent, and had raised a hand to her chest.

"Ha, cat got your tongue? Even you are silent now. Or are you pitying me, thinking this is all really sad? Sorry, but I don't need any of that. I don't think of myself as unfortunate."

I had talked about my life and how I'd grown up with the many women I'd slept with before. When they heard about what happened, some of them would be shocked and withdraw, and some would shower me with pity.

But I believed what I said. I didn't feel like I was unfortunate in any way. Actually I was happy, and felt blessed to be able to live this way. No one else would really get it, though.

Well then, which of the two will this girl be? I narrowed my eyes, awaiting her reaction.

After a long silence, she finally spoke. "…cool."

"Huh?" I didn't understand what she had just said, and was caught off guard. *What's she trying to say? Did I mishear her?* But then…

"I think you're pretty cool, Rufus." There it was again. She said the same thing.

"…What's this all of a sudden? Well, I get that I don't look too shabby, but…" I knew I looked pretty good. But what was this girl going on about after all this time?

"No, I'm not talking about how you look, but how you are on the inside. How you think."

"…The hell is that supposed to mean? I don't get it at all."

"The straightforward way you think… I think it's impressive. And cool." She didn't speak with disgust or rejection, or even pity.

"I just feel that the way you think… is really admirable. It's cool. You should keep living your life just as you are… without ever being swept away by those around you."

They were alike. What she said was just like what that man had said a long, long time ago.

"…Can't believe it. I'm all the way here, and I've met someone who says exactly the same stuff that guy did…?"

It felt like my emotions were flowing back into the past. It was a mysterious feeling, as if something that I had forgotten about long, long ago was suddenly coming back to life.

I turned to face Katarina, only to see her sparkling eyes looking straight at me. *What is with her, really...? What a mysterious girl. Not only strange, but interesting.*

I wondered what she thought as I sat there, all quiet. Now she was staring at me with her mouth agape. I couldn't help myself at the sight of her. I had to laugh.

"Gahahaha!" My previously restrained voice erupted into laughter. I couldn't hold it back anymore — I was struck by waves of laughing, just like back then, when I fooled around with my friends in the slums. "Ha... You're really interesting, you know that? Been a while since I laughed like this."

"Huh..."

It suddenly felt like I was back there, back during those times, riding on a wave of emotions.

"Hey, let's talk some more. I suddenly feel like it'd be good to keep talking."

The more I talked with her, the more I realized just what kind of weirdo Katarina Claes was.

I actually bought the bread in the light meal I'd given her from a bakery in the downtown district. I'd done it out of spite, thinking that I'd insult the noble lady by giving her such food. But as for Katarina...

"Huh?! A bakery downtown? Where exactly is it? It was so delicious! I really must go and buy some next time!" she said, barely concealing her excitement. It seemed like she didn't have a speck of the pride that most nobles had.

And then I found out that her hobbies apparently included tilling fields. She didn't even grow flowers, but instead grew actual crops. And her special skills included fishing and tree-climbing. Honestly, she just seemed like she was some kind of rowdy kid.

Katarina was also very interested in the stories of my travels from when I'd drifted around. I had always lived in the underbellies of society. They weren't good places, so I didn't have any pleasant stories to tell.

Still, she wanted to hear them, and so I told her. I told her about thugs and turf wars, and the dark things I got dragged into, and all that. Any normal girl would find the stories I told terrifying. But Katarina kept nodding with those sparkling eyes of hers. "Amazing, amazing!" she'd say.

Honestly… I felt like this girl was nothing like any other woman I'd met before.

Before I knew it, I was lost in conversation with this girl, and most of the day had gone by. That was when Katarina suddenly, bluntly asked me a question.

"So… come to think of it, since you're not really a butler, does that mean that 'Rufus' is a false name, too?"

Obviously it was, and I told her so. But then she asked what my real name was.

"I have more names than I can count," I responded. "One for each place, you know?"

It was true. In fact, I had so many names that all my fingers and toes couldn't possibly count them all if I tried.

"Then what was your original name?"

The name the man had given me flashed through my mind. "*Sora*," I wanted to say, as Katarina's eyes stared straight into mine. But…

"Don't got one. Unlike you lot, I don't have parents. By the time I even thought about who I was, I was already sifting through trash in the slums."

201

The first name that was given to me by that man… I hadn't used it ever since. But being asked what my actual name was made me think of that name.

I eventually pulled my wandering mind back to reality, and then turned to Katarina once more, only to find her sitting absolutely still.

"Oi! What's with you, clamming up like that? Too traumatic of a conversation for a lady like yourself?"

We'd been talking about some pretty heavy things all this time. I guess hearing about how I don't even have a name gifted to me by my parents was a little too much? But then, Katarina responded completely from left field.

"…really beautiful."

"Huh?" What was this all about, all of a sudden? I didn't get it. I could only stare back, surprised, at Katarina's glittering, aqua-blue eyes.

"Your eyes! Your eyes are really beautiful, like the pure blue sky!"

"…"

"From your beautiful blue eyes; like the sky," was what that man had said to me, a long time ago. The same man who gifted me with the name "Sora."

"I just feel that the way you think… is really admirable. It's cool."

What she said just now was slightly different, but the way she thought about things was so similar to him. It was like I was finally able to meet someone I thought I'd never see again. It was a strange feeling.

I didn't even realize I was doing it, but soon I was holding Katarina in my arms. My heart was overflowing with an emotion I'd never felt before. It was a precious, truly wonderful feeling.

I brushed my fingertips against her soft face, only for her to giggle. I found myself drawn to those pink lips...

Then suddenly, a thunderous sound arose from her belly, jolting me back to reality.

Katarina's blushing face was right in front of me — and I found myself laughing again.

"Guess I'll bring you dinner too, huh."

While I had Katarina moved to another room for dinner because of Selena's wishes yesterday, I decided to have her meal delivered to her room this time. She was a hostage, after all. I couldn't let her just prance around the manor like that.

I had the servants bring dinner to her room... only for her to invite me again. "It's not any fun to eat on my own."

By now, I found myself somewhat comfortable with this girl, and any more objections at this point would probably be kind of silly. I quickly agreed.

"Come to think of it, what happened to Lana? I haven't seen her..."

"Ah, I have her working on some other things. Don't worry about that."

Lana was the maid I hired a while ago. She was an accomplice to this whole plan. She didn't have any living relatives, so it'd be easy to silence her if it ever came down to it. I'd originally hired her only for that reason, but I realized that she was actually very useful when I assigned her some tasks. She did her work well and was tight-lipped. She turned out to be very capable. Right now I was having her look after Selena, whose situation had become a little complicated.

As we started to eat, Katarina once again asked for me to tell her tales from faraway lands, and so I obliged.

"Ha! Honestly Rufus, your stories are so interesting," Katarina said after her meal, seemingly finally satisfied with all she had heard.

"The things you tell me are interesting too. It's too bad you're some nobleman's daughter."

This was my honest opinion. Really, it seemed like having a personality like hers and being a noble lady was probably rough.

"I've never set foot outside this kingdom, but when I'm talking to you, it feels like I've gone on an overseas vacation!"

"Haha, well if it's with you, I feel like I'd like to go visit those places again," I said absently, going along with the conversation. I didn't expect any kind of actual response.

"Really? Then please do take me with you next time!"

My eyes widened in surprise. What the hell was she talking about…? "We live in different worlds, you and me. You know that, right? There's no way I can take you with me."

I wasn't ashamed about my way of life. Even so, I knew very well what kind of person I was, and where I belonged. That was why I understood that once this entire farce was over and done with, I wouldn't be able to spend any more time with this girl.

"Different… worlds? What do you mean? Aren't you sitting before me right now, as you are?" Katarina said, looking straight at me the entire time. "We're talking together, eating together. Doesn't this mean we're in the same world, then?"

Her expression was like she thought I'd said something crazy! Naturally, I found myself laughing in response. "You… really are a strange one, you know that? Okay, I get it. I'll bring you along next time."

Katarina smiled happily at my words. "Okay! It's a promise. Hm… let's pinky promise."

Pinky what now? What's that? Some special cultural gesture in this kingdom I don't know about?

Realizing that I had been mystified by her words, Katarina got up, as if she'd realized something. She then walked towards a dresser tucked away in the corner of the room and promptly fished out her dress from a drawer.

"Here. A symbol of our promise — I am entrusting it to you." With that, she placed something on my hand.

A symbol of promises... that much I knew. A person would give someone a personal possession so that they may hold onto it and give it back the next time they met. There were similar customs in a lot of different countries, but... only children or women who worked in the sex trade still practiced it. In this case, Katarina was definitely doing it the way children did.

I stared at the object in my hands, slightly exasperated. "This is a... brooch?" It looked like it had a stone of some kind embedded in it.

"It is a pretty color, right? It matches your eyes. The blue of the sky." Katarina took the brooch from my hands. "And then... if you tilt it this way so that it catches the light... see? It's aqua-blue now. Like how my eyes are, right?"

Just like she said, as the stone caught the light at a certain angle, the color became exactly like her eyes.

"The color of your eyes, and the color of mine... this brooch is both at the same time! Perfect as a symbol of our promise," Katarina said, smiling faintly.

I had been born with a pretty face, so it was only natural that women came onto me. In fact, I'd never had any problems with women. All kinds would approach me, including hostesses and other "working girls." They'd flirt with familiarity and sweet words, but... I couldn't sense even the slightest hint of that kind of lie in Katarina's words. There was passion in her eyes.

Handing someone a stone that had the colors of both my and her eyes... somehow, it was very convincing. I knew I lived in a different world than the one she lived in. I had steeled myself, knowing that it'd be pointless even if I did want her... and yet. I found my resolve immediately shattered by that one, singular line.

I swept Katarina off her feet, moving her to the bed.

"Being with you... warms me up, you know. Been a while since I felt anything like this."

That warmth was the same feeling I'd lost as a kid. It was a mysterious sensation, and it filled my heart when I was together with this girl.

I took off the glasses I wore, and then pinned her down. Although many women had thrown themselves at me up until now... this was the first time I found myself actually wanting someone.

"Hey... would you like to be mine?"

Although Katarina was pinned down on the bed, for some reason, she was still looking straight up at me with those sparkling eyes of hers. This was the first time anyone had looked at me like that... from such a position. It was nothing like that sappy, needy look that I usually got. My heart was racing.

"If you keep looking at me with your eyes sparkling like that... don't complain if I end up doing... something," I said, nuzzling Katarina's neck as I did so. A fragrant, sweet smell filled my senses. I could no longer resist.

"Um... wait— Rufus...?"

I placed my lips on her soft, white skin... and left my mark upon it. My heart was beating unbelievably fast. Even I couldn't believe what I was feeling.

Up until now, no matter who I slept with, I had never felt anything like this feeling in my heart. If I could have this girl for myself, I...

Bang bang! A few solid knocks sounded through the door.

"Master Rufus, are you available?" a maid's voice inquired loudly.

I clicked my tongue at the interruption. Just when things were going so well…

"I am currently occupied," I said, but whoever was on the other side of the door didn't give in.

"It is quite an urgent matter."

I gave in, partly because of how loud the voice was. There was unshakable resolve in that voice. In the end, I gave in and let Katarina go, then headed towards the door. "Ugh… right when it was getting good, too."

Sighing, I opened the door, only to find the maid that was supposed to be by Selena's side, smiling. "A letter of utmost importance has just arrived for you," she said.

"From whom…?" I asked, without bothering to hide my irritation.

The maid smiled blatantly. "I have left it in your room. Perhaps it would be in your interest to read it as soon as possible," she said, once again with that same smile.

My eyes opened wide. "…You. No… can't be. Well. I guess that's how it is…"

I'd thought that she was simply a maid with no living relatives, and hired her based just on that, but… no. She was more. This maid was probably an agent from some family who had infiltrated this plan from the start. I could tell by the way she was smiling.

After all, I had done nothing but dirty work all these years. My instincts were usually right when it came to things like this. In that case… this plan had already failed.

"…Well. Guess that's that." It was a plan with too many holes anyway.

With a heavy sigh, I left the room.

When I got to my room, the letter was there, as that maid said. It was a letter from Mason.

Apparently, his manor was under investigation. I guess the people at the top finally turned their eyes on him. This time, the small-time crook had gone a little too far. So that meant that everything about this plan must have been revealed already. Mason was never really good at covering his tracks. In that case, the authorities would probably be here soon with the evidence and all that.

There were two paths I could take now. The first option would be to escape from this place as soon as I could. They would surely send people after me, considering that I now had the power of Dark Magic. No matter how I thought about it, running would be a pain in the ass.

The other option was to tell the authorities everything Mason did, his crimes and plots, all the while claiming that I was forced into it. Maybe shed a tear or two.

Circumstances are circumstances, and my life was what it was. Thanks to the hand I'd been dealt, I did have attractive features, and I figured I'd make it out somehow. I might still end up having my life restricted though, which would be frustrating.

Well then… which should I choose? Living my life on the run, or having my freedom restricted…?

"Katarina… psst. Katarina."

"Wah!" Katarina shot away, probably surprised by her late-night guest.

"Haha. You really do sleep well, huh."

"Wh-What do you want?"

"I guess I really put you on your guard, huh. But that's fine. I won't be doing anything anymore. It's time to face the music."

Guess the authorities will be here soon. I haven't seen that maid Lana around either for a while.

"Face… music?"

I told her I had decided that I wouldn't be running after all. My instincts and the experience I'd gained throughout my life agreed with me. Even if I'm restricted with my capture, it would be easier than the alternative.

"Wha?"

"Well… I guess I'll never see you again if I go along with it, so I'm here. Hoping to see your face one last time."

I had messed up plenty of times before now, and I was caught then too. So I felt like things would work out alright. But still… I knew that if I went through with this, I wouldn't be able to see any outsiders — regular, law-abiding people who lived apart from the underbelly of society — for a while. I'd never cared about that until now.

After all, I only made temporary, circumstantial connections with people like that while on a job. At most, there'd be a woman I got a little close to. Even in those cases, I never thought about wanting to see her one last time or anything like that.

I guess things have really changed since meeting this girl, huh... I placed my fingers on Katarina's cheek, savoring the feeling of her soft skin.

"One last time? What do..."

I could hear some kind of commotion outside the room.

"Oh... they're faster than I expected." I withdrew my outstretched hand away from Katarina's cheek and kept my distance from her bed. If that prince who loved and spoiled Katarina so much saw this scene, he'd probably gut me right then and there.

As soon as I'd stepped away, the door slammed open with a loud bang. There was quite the line-up at the door. At the front of it was none other than...

"...Lana?"

The maid merely smiled at Katarina's surprised voice. "Yes. I introduced myself as such a while ago, but I suppose re-introductions are in order. I am Larna Smith, of the Magical Ministry. Raphael's boss. Nice to meet you."

Ah, I see. So this woman was from the Ministry all along. Her presence and aura were completely different from before. She was still the same person from before who I'd dismissed as a plain maid, but now she had an elegant demeanor. Since she could change her presence this much at will, she was definitely no average woman.

And then that not-so-average woman turned towards me and said, "I see that you have chosen to remain... have you steeled yourself for what is to come, then?"

I nodded and said I would tell them everything, making sure to look as meek as possible. That would be important to my "pitiful youth" image.

"Well said. I see your head is in the right place. Without further ado... Rufus Brode. You are hereby under arrest for the kidnap of Lady Katarina Claes. Well then, take him away."

With that, a few of the Ministry flunkies who had been standing behind her surrounded and restrained me. Now it was time for me to be taken away... but before we left, that girl called out to me.

"U-Um!" Katarina said. Her eyes looked desperate.

"I'll hold on to it. Until our promise is fulfilled," I replied, showing her the brooch in my hands.

Katarina seemed reassured by that, and responded cheerfully. "Yes!"

With that, Rufus was taken away, and we were left alone in the room. But Lana, or I guess she was called Larna now, stayed behind.

"Um… Lady Larna? Thank you very much for helping me, and everything you've done for me all this time."

I was amazed that the simple maid turned out to be someone from the Ministry! And from what I just saw, she seemed like someone important too. I thanked her again.

Larna smiled mischievously. "Not at all. Actually, I've always wanted to talk to you. This was all really fun for me."

"Huh? Always?"

Huh? Did she know about me this whole time? I thought in confusion.

Then Raphael spoke up. "Ah, she's the superior I told you about at the school festival, remember?"

Oh, I see. So this is the one who was interested in me all this time? Then… have I met her somewhere before?

"Um, then does that mean we've met before?" I asked. Maybe I'd forgotten someone again?

"Why yes, we have. I didn't look like this when you met me, though, so I wouldn't expect you to recognize me," Larna said with that same smile on her face.

"Look like this…?" *What did she mean?*

Raphael soon offered an explanation. "She is quite the professional at disguises, you see, so she has quite a few looks up her sleeve. She is also the one who taught me how to disguise myself."

What?! So this person before me was the master of disguises I heard about! Amazing! In that case, there was no way I'd remember meeting her before. In fact, I'd probably never recognize her no matter how many times we met! *I wonder how she looked when we met before?*

"If I may ask, how did you look when we met…?"

Larna smiled vaguely. "What you saw was… my exterior."

"Exterior…?" My mind went blank at the word. What did it mean? But then, Larna suddenly hugged me and held me tight.

"Huh? Um.."

"Heheheh. You really are cute, aren't you? I did say I'd hug you the next time we met," Larna said, her blue eyes narrowing like a cat's.

She said she'd hug me the next time we met? Huh? And those eyes… have I seen them somewhere before…?

Just as I was about to remember, Jeord intervened. "That's enough. Return Katarina to me this instant." With that, Jeord pulled me away from Larna's arms.

"Ah, what a short-tempered prince, hmm?" Larna said with a dry laugh.

Hmm… I almost had it, too…

"Katarina, are you alright?" Jeord asked, looking at me with a grave expression.

"Yes, I am totally fine— Ah! That's right! What about Lady Selena? Magic was used on her and…"

I hadn't seen Selena since last night. Rufus had claimed that she was sleeping, but I couldn't help but feel worried.

"Others from the Ministry are currently with Prince Ian, and they are headed to Lady Selena now. There's nothing to worry about," Larna replied.

"Prince Ian is here, too?"

"Yes. He went pale as soon as he heard about all this. This is the first time I've seen him like that, really. It seems like he was really worried about Lady Selena."

"Is that so! That's a relief…" As I thought, you couldn't truly understand things like this without having a conversation about it. It didn't seem like Prince Ian disliked Lady Selena at all, despite what she believed.

"But really, Katarina… it is such a relief that you are alright." Jeord heaved a sigh.

My other friends all said similar things, like, "We're so glad you're safe, Lady Katarina."

"From now on, Big Sister… do be more careful…" Keith said.

"I understand," I said meekly, not sure what else to say.

"Even so… You were kidnapped, Katarina, but for some reason, your skin looks more bright and soft than usual, does it not?" Jeord said, peering at me carefully.

I gulped. Everyone in this room had been so worried, so I couldn't just tell them that my kidnap experience had actually been relaxing and enjoyable.

"I-Is that so…?"

"Yes. Even the sheen of your hair has improved… wait. What is this?" Jeord said, his gaze suddenly stopping on the region around my neck as he ran his fingers through my hair.

"Huh? What is it?"

"This mark on your neck. What exactly is this?"

"Mark? Neck?" *What's he talking about? A mark... Ah! That's right! It's from that time...*

"Oh, this? I was just stung by a bug of some kind."

"An... insect? Stung you?"

"Yes. When Rufus pushed me down onto the bed..."

"Pushed you down onto the bed?!"

Huh? For some reason, Jeord was making a terrifying face. *What's going on?*

"What exactly do you mean, Katarina? So you were pinned down on this bed? Rufus is... the man who was just taken away?"

"Ah, yes. Last night, he suddenly pushed me down. And it seems like a bug stung me then. I thought for sure that he was about to use his magic to put me to sleep, but..."

I had never seen Jeord's expression be so dark and intimidating before. *Someone, please help me...!* With that thought in mind, I looked over to my friends who were standing around us — but for some reason, everyone had equally grave, severe, and intense expressions. *Huh? What? Why? Everyone was full of smiles until just now!*

"It would seem that your definition of 'alright' is quite lacking indeed. Then... other than you being stung by *some insect* after being pinned down, did anything... else, happen?"

"Ah, yes. In the midst of it, Lana— I mean... Lady Larna knocked on the door, and stopped him from casting his magic on me."

Jeord, for some reason, heaved a large sigh. "I had thought that I could match your pace and wait, but it would seem that you could be snatched away at any moment. In that case... I will no longer wait."

"Huh?"

For some reason, Jeord's face was now extremely close to mine. I didn't understand what was going on at all, but... *Ahh, good-looking people are attractive even all close up like this!* That was all I could think.

Before I knew it, Jeord had come so close that I couldn't even see his face anymore. Then I felt a soft, light sensation on my lips. *Wh-What's going on! D-Don't tell me, this is...!*

"I have decided. I shall wait no longer. I could hardly bear it... the thought of someone else taking you for themselves as I wait," said the black-hearted prince who stole my first kiss, smiling.

These lips...! My lips...!

What was this? What's going on? Aren't I just a deterrent against other annoying female suitors? Isn't Jeord actually interested in Maria? Wh-Why a k-kiss, then...?

Apparently the room had erupted into an explosion of noise, but I didn't hear any of it. The thought of that kiss just now filled my mind.

Why? How? What? I couldn't understand it at all...

That was why I, Katarina Claes, who had never had any encounters of the romantic kind in her previous life, had her mind shorted out for the rest of the day. And with that, the curtains finally fell on the kidnapping incident.

★★★★★★★★★

"Selena, Selena."

Someone was desperately calling my name. As I opened my eyes... someone I did not expect to see was at my bedside.

"Prince… Ian?"

"Selena. I see you have awoken. I am relieved." With that, Prince Ian held me tight, as if I were someone he loved. It was like something out of a dream. But his warmth was definitely real.

"I heard everything. I apologize… it was my fault that you went and did that for me." For some reason, Prince Ian was apologizing to me with a heartbroken expression.

"N-No… not at all… It was something I did of my own volition. I acted on my own without thinking… I truly apologize."

Upon waking up, I realized that my mind was now completely clear. And now that I thought about what I did, as I relived the events in my mind, even I was shocked by my actions.

There was no way that I, being Prince Ian's fiancée, wouldn't cause him trouble if I were to be convicted of a crime. I was ashamed of my own foolishness.

"There was nothing that could have been done. You were being controlled. Pay it no heed. More importantly, I am truly relieved that you are safe. I was so worried about you."

Controlled. I thought to ask what Prince Ian meant by that, but the latter half of his statement blew me away.

"Oh… you were worried…? About me?"

"Of course. You are my dear fiancée, after all."

Ah… for Prince Ian to say that I was his dear fiancée… "B-But… do you not hate me, Prince Ian…?"

"If you wish to know the truth, you have to ask Prince Ian, and that's that!" I recalled my promise to Lady Katarina, and decided to ask him the question bluntly.

"What are you saying? Of course I would never feel that way about you," Prince Ian said, looking surprised for reasons unknown to me. It didn't seem like he was lying, however…

"B-But… we hardly see each other, and all this time, you were distant whenever we did meet…" I drew courage from Lady Katarina's words as I continued asking my questions. These were things I had never asked before.

But then, Prince Ian's face reddened. "…Ah."

I wonder what happened…?

"That… is because… you are simply so adorable, and I would not have been able to restrain myself."

"Ah!" I froze upon hearing these unexpected words.

"We are merely engaged. We are not yet formally married. As such, I do not feel that it is appropriate to place my hands upon you when I please. I logically understand that, but… as I gaze upon you… your loveliness compels me to touch you. As such, I felt that it would be for the best for me to see you less often and for me to be somewhat distant from you."

With that, Prince Ian's face reddened some more — it was a shade of deep red that I had never seen in my life.

"However… it would seem like my intentions were misinterpreted. I apologize. Allow me to formally make a declaration. I, Ian Stuart, love you, Selena Berg. I love you very much," Prince Ian said, staring straight at me despite his intensely blushing face.

Ahh… it is just like Lady Katarina said. It was impossible to tell what someone else was thinking about. Only the person in question has the answer, and that was why it was important to have a proper conversation, to talk to each other. It was really just like what Lady Katarina told me.

Overcome with happiness, large tears rolled down my face. Prince Ian quickly wiped each one away with his fingers, all the while fidgeting in concerned embarrassment.

★★★★★★★★★

With the Katarina Claes kidnapping incident resolved, and a report to the Magical Ministry turned in, I found myself holding a copy of said report and walking towards my partner's room.

I stopped in front of his door. "I'm coming in," I said.

"Feel free," was his response. He turned to face me as I entered his room with that flippant look of his, as always. "Ah! I see that today, of all days, you have made yourself quite plain indeed!"

"Of course. I was disguised as a simple maid with no living relatives. I did have a wig on, though." I lifted the brown wig off my head, allowing my natural black hair to reveal itself.

"No matter how many times I see them, I must say. Your disguises are really impressive, Susanna Randall."

"I am most honored by your praise, Prince Jeffrey," I responded to the casually smiling prince in a dignified, ladylike manner.

The professional disguise master of the Magical Ministry, Larna Smith, was none other than Susanna Randall — fiancée of Prince Jeffrey, first prince of the kingdom.

Other than Prince Jeffrey himself, only those that stood at the top echelons of the Ministry knew about my true identity. As to why I had disguised myself, and why I used a false name… well, I couldn't simply continue casually working at the Ministry as Susanna, after all.

It was because I had hidden my identity that I was able to accept Jeffrey's request in the first place. It was none other than Jeffrey himself who had picked up on Marquess Mason's strange behavior, and then made the request for me to look into this kidnapping. As a result, we were able to resolve the incident quickly.

The man known as Jeffrey Stuart was, despite his appearance, very capable at his work. If anything, his flippant behavior was a front that allowed him to move quietly behind the scenes.

Actually, David Mason was one of Jeffrey's supporters. As for why a man who had so many dark rumors swirling around him was allowed into Jeffrey's political factions... well, by allowing these individuals into his political sphere, Jeffrey hoped to dig up the dirt on these people — and once the evidence was on hand, they could be summarily destroyed.

Jeffrey had purposely taken in people like Mason so as to prevent them from infiltrating Ian's camp. As a result, there were many questionable individuals in Jeffrey's sphere of influence. Even so, he hardly minded, and was in fact satisfied with this arrangement. Yes, Jeffrey Stuart had never really cared for the crown. He had but one wish.

As soon as I finished delivering my report on the incident at hand...

"Hmm. Even so, though. Someone like Mason scurrying around in the dark, and then going after Ian and Jeord... unforgivable. I suppose we will really have to... utterly, completely, crush him, then," Jeffrey said, a dark smile coming over his features.

Just looking at his expression was enough to tell me that Mason was done. If he had just stuck to the small-time crimes that were his specialty, then perhaps he would have been penalized accordingly. But to lay his hands on Jeffrey's brothers, of all things... surely, an unimaginable punishment awaited this man.

"Ah, but I'm glad that it all ended without event! So tell me... are my wonderful brothers doing well?" Prince Jeffrey asked, the previously dark smile on his face now replaced with a pleasant one.

"Yes. Well indeed."

"Good to know!" With that, Jeffrey jumped out of his chair, ran towards the wall, and drew back the curtains that hung there. "Ahh, my brothers are truly, truly wonderful."

Jeffrey approached the now-exposed wall — and hung on it were the portraits of the other three princes. This part of his room, which was usually concealed by curtains, displayed these portraits proudly.

Indeed, with this it was easy to see that the true nature of this man was that of a complete freak — one that loved his brothers dearly... and intensely. Only a few people knew of this side of him, and I was one of them.

To cover this up, he participated in the struggle for the crown against Ian — all an act, of course. In this charade of a struggle, he would absorb criminals and ne'er-do-wells into his own sphere, secretly ensuring that no ill elements wandered into Ian's faction. He was also constantly on the alert, ensuring that no strange individuals approached his younger twin brothers.

Jeffrey Stuart only had one wish — for his beloved brothers to happily live in peace. To that end, this deviant prince would pull out all the stops. Yes, he would really do anything.

When I had first met him as his fiancée, I said the following to him: "I am not interested in anything but the research of magic. I have no interest in being your queen." And that was my greeting.

Jeffrey, however, had something of his own to say. "I am not interested in anything but my brothers. I have no intent to actually claim the throne, either."

Ah. It was a good memory, now that I thought about it. It had been ten or so years since that first meeting... and for some reason, I got along with this freak here swimmingly. I lived my life in service to the Ministry, and him in service to his brothers. We both continued our passion of arresting criminals in the kingdom — and those were our days. I had this freak to thank, somewhat, for allowing me to quickly dodge the annoyances of marriage and the like, and do whatever I wanted at the Ministry.

Jeffrey continued staring at the portraits. "Ahh… those eyes. Just like mine." Again and again he mouthed off these incomprehensible statements, lost in his own world. A true deviant indeed.

I supposed he would not be coming back to reality anytime soon… and so I helped myself to some tea in the room that had been prepared beforehand. *Hmm, as expected of tea meant for the lips of royals. Delicious.*

Anyway, this Katarina Claes was a really interesting girl, even though I was never one to develop this kind of interest in people. It all started back when the two younger twin princes had their birthday party. I had become weary of all the forced interactions, and had been resting in a corner when… she started eating. At an alarming speed.

Next, she started gulping down a cup of wine, quickly got drunk, and then turned the cup upside-down in her confusion. I hadn't expected to see something like this at a party held within the castle walls. I was surprised… and that was when I developed an interest in this girl.

As I continued looking into her, I heard more and more interesting things. Although I had only met her once, I was already intrigued by her.

We did meet at the school festival once more, but she hardly said anything to me — imagine how lonely that was! But by a sheer stroke of luck, Katarina appeared in my infiltration mission, and I was able to speak with her to my heart's content.

Now that I had gotten the chance to actually speak to Katarina for an extended period of time, I quickly realized that she was infinitely more interesting and wonderful than I thought.

Ahh... I simply must have Katarina Claes join the Ministry, and be within reach.

As I continued indulging in my thoughts, I couldn't help but notice that my expression began to resemble Jeffrey's as he continued staring at the portraits on the wall.

★★★★★★★★★★

Now that everything was safely resolved, I returned to the academy's dormitory.

But after all that happened, I felt like I'd had some kind of strange dream. My memories of what had happened towards the end of everything were muddled, and I only heard about it from Keith later.

I suppose it was simply because I didn't sleep well due to the kidnapping, and that was why I had a dream like that. Hmm... yes. That had to be it. Though actually, it would be more likely that the problem was me sleeping too much. Maybe.

In any case, everything was wrapped up in the end. From what I had heard, the mastermind was a marquess by the name of David Mason. He had done it so that Prince Jeffrey could take over the throne, but the prince himself seemed oblivious to this.

I suppose that Great Detective Katarina's deductions were somewhat off, but personally I was glad that the brothers didn't fight amongst themselves.

Also... Rufus, who had obtained the powers of Dark Magic at Mason's orders, was now being confined at the Magical Ministry.

From what I heard, Rufus spilled the beans on Mason's operations, plans, and misdeeds, and was claiming that he was forced into it — all the while shedding plenty of tears.

Rufus' case was helped by the fact that he came from unfortunate circumstances. In the end, he would not be charged for any of these crimes, and would instead remain in the protective custody of the Ministry, much like Raphael.

Honestly, I didn't feel that Rufus was all that unfortunate, and he wasn't crying intensely when I was speaking to him. I guess he did well hiding his true feelings.

Keith, however, strongly disagreed. "He should be charged with much heavier crimes!"

Although the two hadn't met for very long at all, Keith seemed to perceive Rufus as an enemy of some kind. I wonder why?

But the most surprising thing that greeted me when I returned to the academy was the fact that I had been awarded a Merit Award of Excellence.

The Merit Award was a recognition that was handed out to several students at the end of the school festival for outstanding creations, productions, displays of ability and things like that. One of these awards was given to me for my role in the student council's play. Apparently my performance had been intense and intimidating, and everyone had loved it.

On another note, Maria's homemade snacks were very popular too, and she was also chosen to receive some sort of award. That's my Maria!

These were honorary awards, so they didn't have any kind of prize or anything. But even so, being chosen for an award like that was a truly honorable thing in the academy. Maria was one thing, but for me to be chosen too? It was a really satisfying achievement.

Though in the end, I guess that meant I'd always be the childhood-friend archetype villainess no matter what I did.

I planned to present the award to my parents when I went home to the manor during my next school break. Although my father was busy with his work and my parents hadn't been able to come to the school festival, I was sure they'd be happy to see it.

After all this, my life at the Academy of Magic went back to normal — although still with some surprises here and there.

Keith had recently become a lot more protective of me. He would follow me everywhere I went. Well, actually Keith wasn't the only one. All my other friends were like that too, to the point where I started wondering if the council work was being done at all.

Of course, I understood that my friends would be worried since I'd been kidnapped and all that. But even so, they were going above and beyond. Even I needed some time to myself.

So that evening, I silently sneaked out of the dorms and headed in the direction of the fields. When I got there, I saw someone who, unlike my other friends, had hardly shown himself since the kidnapping.

"Prince Jeord."

"Ah. Katarina. Together again at last." Jeord approached me with a pleasant smile, but I found myself nervous at the sight of him alone.

This was because of the strange dream I'd had after the kidnapping. In that dream, I was kissing Jeord, of all people. Why would I have a dream like that? Was it because I hadn't had any romance in my life, and was feeling pent up? That's so embarrassing...

I had hardly seen Jeord since then and had almost forgotten about it, but now that he was standing in front of me, I couldn't help but remember it and feel nervous.

225

Jeord had no idea what I was thinking of course, and he soon enveloped me in his arms. That was fine, I guess. Though now that I thought about it, his displays of friendliness were pretty intense. *Is it because he's a prince?*

Ah, this is why I keep feeling so pent up, and why I had a dream like that! Ugh... I see. It's all Jeord's fault.

"So much has gotten between us. It has been most lonely being without you, my beloved princess."

Those last words were what Jeord, playing the role of the prince, said to Maria's heroine in the council's play. They were sweet words, yes, but there wasn't much of a difference between that and what Jeord said normally. He was always talking like that; in fact, he often whispered things in my ear, like he was doing now.

This was how it always was... but hearing such suggestive words right in my ear made my face heat up. Maybe it was because of my dream. I couldn't look at Jeord normally anymore, and instead felt flustered and embarrassed.

For some reason, Jeord's eyes seemed to sparkle as he saw my hesitation. "Oh, quite the rare response, Katarina. I suppose even you would become aware of it, given what has recently transpired...?"

Hmm? Recently? What does he mean? "Huh? Ah... no. I just had a strange dream the other day..."

"A dream?"

"Yes... a dream where you and I, uh..."

It's no good! I was overwhelmed with embarrassment and couldn't find the words. I could only feel my voice rumbling, stuck in my throat, and my cheeks were burning up. My eyes were practically spinning! I was looking around nervously, and almost felt like I was going to tear up.

After all, I had zero experience with romance in my previous life! I hadn't even had the chance to talk about love and all that stuff with my friends! *Ugh... If only this were happening in a two-dimensional space! I could handle it then.*

But to have an impossibly handsome prince who looked like he'd just stepped out of a fairy tale staring at me at such a close range, all while I was thinking about the word "kiss"... I could barely even speak! And anyway, if I told him something like that, I'm sure he'd see me as a disgusting, desperate person, which would be even more embarrassing!

But for some reason, Jeord looked delighted at the sight of my currently shaken self. I wondered if he realized it, but his cheeks were red now too. *Huh? But why? Did my embarrassment spread to him?*

"Hmm. So, Katarina... pray tell, what kind of dream was it?" Jeord asked with a blissful expression. And then, just like in that dream, he moved his face close to mine... and I suddenly felt a soft sensation on my lips. This was...!

"Mm!" An exclamation from me finally made the strange object move from my lips, but Jeord simply continued laughing, as if he was pleased.

"So you thought it was a dream? But I assure you... what happened just now, and what happened then — neither of those were dreams."

"B-But why?" *I'm only Jeord's fiancée so he can ward off other ladies, right? Why would he kiss me then? Is he just messing with me? Actually, wait! Isn't Jeord a character who has that kind of personality?!*

"I presume you are asking about the kiss? But of course, Katarina, it is because I love you so."

"Huh?!" *L-Love?! What does he mean by love? That...*

Jeord placed a hand on my face and grinned, and I felt like I was going to melt into a puddle. "Haha... So you have noticed it at last? Ah, Katarina. I am very happy indeed."

Lost in my confusion, I could see Jeord's face approaching mine once more...

"Hold it right there! Don't you dare get any nearer to Big Sister!"

"Please, move out of the way, Master Keith. I fully intend to start with a round of attack spells..."

"W-Wait, Mary! What do you think you're doing!"

"Oh... no, Lady Mary... do allow me..."

"Lady S-Sophia... please calm down. It would be very dangerous to send anything of the sort flying in their direction... At the very least, please make sure the injuries are of a degree that I could heal..."

Before I knew it, everyone had showed up. I was snatched away from Jeord and pushed behind them all, and after that, it seemed like the chaos wasn't going to end anytime soon. Everyone was speaking at once! It was a cacophony of voices, but not a single word entered my ears.

He said that he loved me, though... d-does this mean that it was a confession?! And this wasn't even my first kiss... but my second?

I had been proposed to despite having no brushes with romance in my previous and current life? Kissed, too? And on top of all that, my partner was none other than a handsome prince from an otome game!

To begin with, Jeord was an impossibly difficult character to romance! Even Maria, who was a wonderful character herself, had difficulty doing so in the game. There was no way this could be really happening.

Perhaps this is a dream after all! With that thought in mind, I gave myself a good pinch… and it hurt a lot. It would seem that this was reality after all.

As I stood there, stunned, I felt like I heard a familiar voice — the elated voice of my best friend from my previous life: *"Congratulations on successfully romancing the black-hearted prince!"*

Cinderellamaria
and
the Villainess-Faced Stepsister

Art: Nami Hidaka

Cast

Cinderella — Maria
Stepsister — Katarina
Prince 1 — Jeord
Prince 2 — Alan

Note: This comic is a parody based on the Cinderella-like play that was performed in the main story.
Another Note: While the panels retain their original right to left order, the pages go left to right
for consistency with the rest of the book.

One day, a ball was held at the royal castle.

KATARINA RULES ☆

She was bullied every day by her step-mother and step-sister.

Once, there was a beautiful girl by the name of Maria.

SLUMP

Nothing to wear to the ball.

But poor Maria had no nice shoes or dresses...

...

Maria's step-mother and step-sister were over-joyed!

However, the next morning —

How amazing!

TO: ☆ MARIA ☆

Wonderful presents were laid out by her bedside when she awoke!

And so, Maria was able to attend the ball at the castle.

KYAAAAH!

The stars of the event were the twin princes of the castle.

The purpose of the ball was for the princes to find brides.

IT'S TIRING, HAVING SO MANY PEOPLE HERE. AS LONG AS SHE MEETS THE CONDITIONS, MY BRIDE COULD BE ANYONE...

ohh, this is good too!

SNATCH

DELICIOUS!♥

?!

HOW POINT-LESS.

IT'S THE SAME BORING THING EVERY DAY.

RUSTLE RUSTLE

GLANCE GLANCE

WHERE DID THAT GIRL GO?

AH...

I'M SURE I SAW HER SOME-WHERE AROUND HERE...

I'M SORRY...

W-WAIT!

WHAT'S WITH THAT SMILE?!

GUH!

THUD!

And so the prince found a single shoe, which he'd use to find his bride!

A month passed since the ball...

AH, MARIA'S COOKING IS DELICIOUS!

SHE'S GENTLE AND CUTE! IF I WERE THE PRINCE, I WOULD SURELY TAKE MARIA AS MY BRIDE!

Cinderella-Maria's stepsister, Katarina, adored Maria's cooking.

COME TO THINK OF IT...

munch

munch

munch

KNOCK
KNOCK
KNOCK

COMING!

THOUGH IF HE WAS A PRINCE, I'D DEFINITELY BE ARRESTED FOR CONTEMPT OF ROYALTY... LIKE THAT'D EVER HAPPEN!

HE WAS REALLY SPARKLY AND HANDSOME.

HIS SMILE WAS SO SCARY I RAN AWAY IMMEDIATELY...

I WONDER IF THAT GUY IS OKAY? THE ONE I DROPPED MY SHOE ON.

TA-DA!

EEK!

YOU—

AND WHO MIGHT...

And so it came to be that the villainess-faced stepsister ~~was captured~~ fell for the prince at first sight, and became his fiancée.

And they lived happily ever after!

AH, BECAUSE YOU ARE INTERESTING.

BUT WHY?

BUT WOULD YOU COME BACK TO THE CASTLE WITH ME AND BECOME MY BRIDE?

HM...? I KNOW NOT OF WHAT YOU SPEAK,

I-IT CAN'T BE! CONTEMPT OF ROYALTY? REALLY?!

CLUTCH

Hello. This is Satoru Yamaguchi. Thank you very much for purchasing my book. This is the third volume of *My Next Life as a Villainess: All Routes Lead to Doom!*

I had originally planned to finish the series with two volumes, but I was able to complete the third volume as well thanks to everyone's support. I would like to express my heartfelt thanks.

The third volume contains the new adventures of the protagonist, Katarina, after she has safely dodged all the Catastrophic Bad Ends. New characters are also being featured and illustrated. I would be very happy if you enjoyed this volume.

I would also like to express my gratitude towards Nami Hidaka-sama, for their beautiful and wonderful illustrations across the volumes. Thank you very much.

Last but not least, I would like to thank the supervisor of the publishing department, who gave me a lot of advice as I sat, fidgeting nervously at the prospect of writing a new novel. I would also like to offer my heartfelt thanks to everyone who has helped me in some way or form, eventually allowing this book to be published.

Thank you very much, everyone.

Satoru Yamaguchi

2

COMPLETE SERIES
ON SALE NOW!

Author: **Ameko Kaeruda**
Illustrator: **Kazutomo Miya**

SEXILED

My Sexist Party Leader Kicked Me Out,
o I Teamed Up With a Mythical Sorceress

ASCENDANC
OF A
BOOKWOR

I'll do anything to
become a libraria

Part 2 **Apprentice Shrir
Maiden Vol. 3**

Author: **Miya Kazuki**
Illustrator: **You Shiina**

PART 1 VOLUMES 1-3
& PART 2 VOLUMES 1-4
ON SALE NOW!

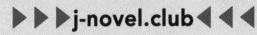

J-Novel Club Lineup

Ebook Releases Series List

A Lily Blooms in Another World
A Wild Last Boss Appeared!
Altina the Sword Princess
Amagi Brilliant Park
An Archdemon's Dilemma:
    How to Love Your Elf Bride
Arifureta Zero
Arifureta: From Commonplace
    to World's Strongest
Ascendance of a Bookworm
Beatless
Bibliophile Princess
Black Summoner
By the Grace of the Gods
Campfire Cooking in Another
    World with My Absurd Skill
Can Someone Please Explain
    What's Going On?!
Cooking with Wild Game
Crest of the Stars
Deathbound Duke's Daughter
Demon Lord, Retry!
Der Werwolf: The Annals of Veight
From Truant to Anime Screenwriter:
    My Path to "Anohana" and "The
    Anthem of the Heart"
Full Metal Panic!
Grimgar of Fantasy and Ash
Her Majesty's Swarm
Holmes of Kyoto
How a Realist Hero Rebuilt the
    Kingdom
How NOT to Summon a Demon
    Lord
I Refuse to Be Your Enemy!
I Saved Too Many Girls and Caused
    the Apocalypse
I Shall Survive Using Potions!
In Another World With My
    Smartphone
Infinite Dendrogram
Infinite Stratos
Invaders of the Rokujouma!?
Isekai Rebuilding Project
JK Haru is a Sex Worker in Another
    World
Kobold King
Kokoro Connect
Last and First Idol
Lazy Dungeon Master
Mapping: The Trash-Tier Skill That
    Got Me Into a Top-Tier Party

Middle-Aged Businessman, Arise in
    Another World!
Mixed Bathing in Another
    Dimension
Monster Tamer
My Big Sister Lives in a Fantasy
    World
My Instant Death Ability is So
    Overpowered, No One in This
    Other World Stands a Chance
    Against Me!
My Next Life as a Villainess: All
    Routes Lead to Doom!
Otherside Picnic
Outbreak Company
Outer Ragna
Record of Wortenia War
Seirei Gensouki: Spirit Chronicles
Sexiled: My Sexist Party Leader
    Kicked Me Out, So I Teamed Up
    With a Mythical Sorceress!
Slayers
Sorcerous Stabber Orphen:
    The Wayward Journey
Tearmoon Empire
Teogonia
The Bloodline
The Combat Butler and Automaton
    Waitress
The Economics of Prophecy
The Epic Tale of the Reincarnated
    Prince Herscherik
The Extraordinary, the Ordinary,
    and SOAP!
The Greatest Magicmaster's
    Retirement Plan
The Holy Knight's Dark Road
The Magic in this Other World is
    Too Far Behind!
The Master of Ragnarok & Blesser
    of Einherjar
The Sorcerer's Receptionist
The Tales of Marielle Clarac
The Underdog of the Eight Greater
    Tribes
The Unwanted Undead Adventurer
WATARU!!! The Hot-Blooded
    Fighting Teen & His Epic
    Adventures in a Fantasy World
    After Stopping a Truck with His
    Bare Hands!!

The White Cat's Revenge as
    Plotted from the Demon Ki
    Lap
The World's Least Interesting
    Master Swordsman
Welcome to Japan, Ms. Elf!
When the Clock Strikes Z
Wild Times with a Fake Fake
    Princess

Manga Series:

A Very Fairy Apartment
An Archdemon's Dilemma:
    How to Love Your Elf Bride
Animeta!
Ascendance of a Bookworm
Bibliophile Princess
Black Summoner
Campfire Cooking in Another
    World with My Absurd Skill
Cooking with Wild Game
Demon Lord, Retry!
Discommunication
How a Realist Hero Rebuilt the
    Kingdom
I Love Yuri and I Got Bodyswa
    with a Fujoshi!
I Shall Survive Using Potions!
Infinite Dendrogram
Mapping: The Trash-Tier Skill
    Got Me Into a Top-Tier Par
Marginal Operation
Record of Wortenia War
Seirei Gensouki: Spirit Chronic
Sorcerous Stabber Orphen:
    The Reckless Journey
Sorcerous Stabber Orphen:
    The Youthful Journey
Sweet Reincarnation
The Faraway Paladin
The Magic in this Other World
    Too Far Behind!
The Master of Ragnarok & Ble
    of Einherjar
The Tales of Marielle Clarac
The Unwanted Undead Adven

Keep an eye out at j-novel.club
    for further new title
    announcements!